FAVRE
THE TOTAL PACKAGE

from the publisher of
Sports Collectors Digest

©2008 Krause Publications

Published by

krause publications

An Imprint of F+W Publications

700 East State Street • Iola, WI 54990-0001
715-445-2214 • 888-457-2873
www.krausebooks.com

Our toll-free number to place an order or obtain
a free catalog is (800) 258-0929.

Library of Congress Control Number: 2008931934

ISBN-13: 978-0-89689-840-0
ISBN-10: 0-89689-840-7

Designed by Tom Nelsen
Edited by Paul Kennedy

Front & Back Cover: Courtesy David Stluka/Getty Images

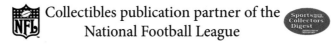
Collectibles publication partner of the
National Football League

Printed in the United States of America

Contents

Foreword

BY BOB HARLAN

**Bob Harlan, Green Bay Packers
Chairman Emeritus**

It was an honor to watch Brett Favre play.

I have always felt that way. Over the years I have told people the day will come when we will say how fortunate we were to have seen Brett play and to witness his wonderful career. I've always maintained that the last time he went down the tunnel and onto the field at Lambeau it would be a sad day for the Green Bay Packers and a sad day for the National Football League.

Brett is an icon. There won't be another player like him.

He brought a child-like enthusiasm to the game. Brett had fun. I think fans appreciated that.

Yet there were many things fans didn't see. Brett played the toughest and most demanding position in football, both mentally and physically. I would see him in the locker room after the game and he could hardly move. There were times I would see him during the week and he could hardly move. But on Sunday he would run out of the tunnel ready to go and ready to compete.

I marveled at that. I thought that was wonderful. Of all the records Brett holds, and he holds some magnificent records, the one that impresses me the most is that he was there every single Sunday to play.

I have always said and I will always maintain that the foundation that restored this franchise to the elite in the National Football League in the 1990s was Ron Wolf, Mike Holmgren, Brett Favre and Reggie White. I find it sad that none of them are here anymore.

People often ask me about my favorite moment of Brett's career. I really think it was the first touchdown in Super Bowl XXXI when he threw to Andre Rison and he ran off the field with his helmet off. He looked like a kid running home to his mother with his first great report card

I was so nervous about us being at the Super Bowl. But after that throw, and after watching him run off the field like that I had a great deal of confidence. That was a great feeling I will never forget. I've always told people Brett plays with a sandlot enthusiasm for the game, and you don't see that very often. The league is going to miss that.

I understand the pressures of being Brett Favre and living up to what our fans expected of him. I wish him well. It was a privilege to watch him. I truly mean that. I talk to people who say, "I watched Babe Ruth" or "I watched Lou Gehrig" or "I watched Johnny Blood."

Well, we watched Brett Favre. That's pretty good.

Introduction

BY BRIAN EARNEST
Editorial Director, Sports Collectors Digest

It was a beautiful, sun-drenched Sunday at Lambeau Field. The fans were in short sleeves and the free-wheeling Bengals were in town for what figured to be an entertaining battle with the Packers. The date was Sept. 20, 1992.

And then, in the blink of an eye, all the air seemed to go out of the stadium. The Packers' popular quarterback, Don Majkowski, rolled an ankle and, suddenly, things didn't look too promising for the home team – not only for the game, but possibly for the rest of the season.

And then in strolls some guy wearing No. 4 with a funny last name: F-A-V-R-E. Even the Packer faithful didn't seem to really know who the guy was. "How is that pronounced again? 'Fav-ray?' Where did this guy come from? Oh yeah, he's that backup quarterback we blew a No. 1 pick on in that trade with Atlanta."

Well, the new guy spent most of that afternoon running in circles, dropping snaps, making up his own plays and generally conducting his own unscripted fire drill. But he also threw rockets all over the field, completed a touchdown pass to Sterling Sharpe, then pulled off the first of many miracles in his career when he fired a game-winning TD pass in the final seconds to unknown wideout Kitrick Taylor. The denizens of Lambeau went wild. Favre went wild. It was a crazy scene.

Yes, the Fav-ray kid turned out to be pretty good. Only a few hard-core fans knew who he was before that day, but it wasn't long before everybody across the NFL knew. Certainly, none of the 60,000-plus on hand that day could have any idea that No. 4 would hardly ever leave the field for the next 16 years. He started the next week — a win against the powerful Steelers — and never missed a game for the rest of his unbelievable career.

Those of us who were in the Lambeau stands on that gorgeous fall day will never forget it. And we won't forget the 16 falls, three MVPs and countless miracles that followed.

We hope you enjoy this tribute to Brett Favre, one of the greatest players in NFL history, and one of the most colorful and entertaining sports figures of any era. He made us gasp, laugh, cry, cheer, shake our heads and shout at the TV. He was a true original — seemingly equal parts John Wayne, John Elway, Huckleberry Finn and the goofy kid from your high school home room. He was a Wrangler-wearing Everyman. A hero with razor stubble on his chin and mischief on his mind. And his exploits were matched only by his Hall of Fame personality.

This book was made possible through the efforts of many talented people. No one's contributions are more appreciated than the behind-the-scenes work of Chris Havel. Havel, the author of two best-selling Favre autobiograhies, provided invaluable insight and direction to the book.

"I never stepped onto the field or walked off a field where I didn't feel like I did everything I could possibly do to be the best."
— Brett Favre

The Numbers Don't Lie

Yet The Records Favre Set Can't Fully Explain His Greatness

BY PAUL KENNEDY

You can get lost in the numbers. The touchdown passes, the wins, the playing streak, the awards. Amazing, mind-boggling numbers. But like mirrors in a carnival funhouse, they reflect greatness as well as distort it.

We play a silly game when measuring our sports heroes. It's not enough that a football player has a great career, a record-setting career, even a Hall-of-Fame career. No, we are compelled to compare him to all others who have ever played the game.

The Greatest of All-Time. That's what we so passionately argue. Our yardstick? Numbers. As if statistics and records have anything to do with transcendence.

If they did, the argument would be short. By the end of his career, Brett Favre held nearly every meaningful passing record in National Football League history. He stands as the league's only three-time Most Valuable Player, winning the award in 1995, 1996 and 1997. And at 38 — an age when most players have been retired for years — Favre enjoyed one of the best seasons of his storied career.

The numbers are indeed heady. The thing is, if you're a fan looking to measure the greatness of Brett Favre, you don't start with the head. You start with the heart. First his. Then yours.

That's why this story isn't so much about numbers as it is about pictures.

It is March 1997. Deanna Favre sets the box of family photo albums on the bed of a Hattiesburg, Miss., hotel room. Only a few months before, Deanna's husband had led the Green Bay Packers to their first Super Bowl victory in 29 years. Now she's asked to provide family photographs to be featured in her husband's autobiography. The book — *Favre: For the Record* — would be released that fall and become the best-selling sports book of the year.

I had not met Deanna before that day, although I certainly knew who she was. I was in Hattiesburg with longtime friend and former *Green Bay Press-Gazette* sportswriter Chris Havel, helping him write Favre's book. The idea for the book was hatched in 1993 when Havel approached Favre three days into his second training camp with the Packers.

"Brett, I think you might have a book in you someday," Havel said one day after practice. "How do you feel about getting together to write one when the time comes?"

At the time, Favre had a mere 14 NFL starts under his belt. Still, the request didn't faze him. He had only one question: "Who are we going to write about?"

> *Brett Favre rewrote the NFL record books during a magical 17-year career. Still, the debate about the best quarterback of all-time centers not on numbers but something immeasurable, and much more human.*

Havel laughed and Favre smiled. Then they shook hands. And that was that. The entire conversation lasted less than two minutes. Four years later, with Favre having won two MVP awards and a Super Bowl ring, there were all sorts of suitors clamoring to tell his story. The quarterback stuck with Havel. Loyalty is one of his more endearing traits.

The Images

One of the first photographs Deanna shares was taken from the deck of the Favre's childhood home in Kiln, Miss. To say that Kiln is a small town is to give it the benefit of the doubt. There just isn't much there. Curley Hallman, Favre's old coach at the University of Southern Mississippi, once described Kiln as "a place that's kind of like the *Dukes of Hazzard* minus the demolition derby."

Favre's family home was about 12 miles from the Gulf of Mexico and so close to the Rotten Bayou that you could spit into it off their deck. Favre had four dogs growing up. One was a chocolate Labrador retriever named Lucky, who, it turned out, wasn't. Neither were the others. Alligators got them all.

Both of Favre's parents were teachers. His mother, Bonita, taught special education. His father, Irvin — or Big Irv, as everyone knew him — taught physical education and drivers education at Hancock North Central High School. A lot of kids at Hancock learned how to do push-ups and parallel park under Big Irv's tutelage. Big Irv also coached football. All three of his sons — Scott, Brett and Jeff — played quarterback for him at Hancock. Brett was blessed with the strong arm. His little sister Brandi got the good looks: she was once named Miss Teen Mississippi.

Infectious joy

Deanna pulls out a picture. It's from Bonita Favre. In the black-and-white photo, Brett wears No. 10 for the Hancock North Central High Hawks football team. He is a sophomore, and by the size of the grin on his face he's having the time of his life. It's pure joy. The kid just can't help himself.

That grin followed him from Hancock to Green Bay. You've seen it a thousand times.

There were quarterbacks like Joe Montana and Steve Young that may have been equal or better than Favre at running the complex West Coast offense. There were quarterbacks like Fran Tarkenton and Randall Cunningham who were better scramblers. And there were quarterbacks like Johnny Unitas and John Elway with perhaps even

stronger arms. Maybe Joe Namath and Montana were more famous for grace under pressure. But Favre has all these qualities in abundance. But more importantly, he has another trait that transcends physical skills — infectious joy.

Peyton Manning and Tom Brady are wonderful quarterbacks. Both will assuredly end up in the Hall of Fame. By all accounts they seem like good guys. Manning's many TV commercials are even amusing. But really, when was the last time you saw either one of them play as if they were having fun on the field? Brady's self-satisfied smirk doesn't count as joyful. Manning, despite his commercials, still comes off as business-like. Effective? You bet. Like a surgeon, and just as sterile.

To have your hero do something amazing on the field, and then to have him celebrate the achievement with whoops and hollers and unabashed giddiness — that, my friend, is to have a hero to cherish for life. I have yet to see Manning lift receiver Marvin Harrison onto his shoulders and run with him after a touchdown pass. Favre has hoisted Donald Driver so many times you would think he was a firefighter saving him from a burning building. Does that make Favre a better quarterback? No. Just a lot more fun to watch.

The Business Arrangement

Every photograph Deanna brings has a story. There's Brett and James "Bus" Cook. The two are wearing tuxedos at an award ceremony honor-

ing Favre. Cook is Favre's longtime agent. When they met, Cook was a lawyer in Hattiesburg. Favre was playing for Southern Mississippi. When Favre asked him to be his agent, Cook said, "I don't know. I've never been an agent." To which Favre replied, "That's OK, I've never been a professional quarterback." The two were made for each other.

While working on Favre's autobiography, we were invited to Cook's home, which was under construction outside of Hattiesburg. It was dark when we arrived. Cook, Favre and a couple of his high school buddies were shooting the breeze while standing around a pile of burning brush.

At one point, Favre stood in the bucket of the front-end loader Cook had used to clear the brush and questioned his agent's building ability. The next thing anyone knew, Cook hopped behind the controls of the rig and hoisted his prized client about six feet up in the air. He wouldn't let him down until Favre apologized for the perceived insult to his manhood. That or he was just tired of listening to Favre talk smart. Everyone howled, including a future Hall of Fame quarterback perched high overhead in the bucket of a front-end loader.

So the answer is yes. The goofiness you see from Favre is genuine, and it is not limited to the football field.

Brett and Deanna

Deanna pages through another photo album, stopping when she comes across a photo of her and Brett. They're dressed up for his high

> *"If they were looking for a symbol for toughness in the dictionary they'd get Brett Favre."*
>
> — Willlie Davis,
> Packers Hall of Fame defensive end

school junior prom. He is in a white tuxedo and blue bow tie, and she in a white dress. The photo could be of just about any high school kids in America. Funny, but that moment must seem like a million years ago now; so much has happened. Most of it played out for all of us to see.

Back then it was pretty simple. They were high school sweethearts. Both were good athletes: She an all-conference basketball player and he a star football and baseball player. Usually the two just hung out together, talking and playing some kind of sport. Brett was a pitcher on the baseball team, and for fun Deanna would catch him. That's how they spent time together, with Brett firing fastballs at her and Deanna never backing down.

It seems that early practice of taking everything Brett could throw at her would pay off down the road.

Throughout his 17-year career, that shy, small-town girl has been by his side, yet somehow in the shadows. Fame, fortune, deaths in the family, the addiction to painkillers that threatened Brett's career, and the ensuing 46-day stint in drug rehab that saved it — they dealt with a lot.

When Walter Iooss, the famed photographer for *Sports Illustrated*, photographed Favre for the cover of his autobiography as well as for a *Got Milk?* ad campaign, the young quarterback's hair was dark. Ten years later, it's mostly gray. There's a reason.

In 2004, Deanna was diagnosed with breast cancer. When treatment caused her hair to fall out, Brett shaved his head in support. Deanna emerged cancer free and has written a candid and inspirational memoir, *Don't Bet Against Me: Beating the Odds of Breast Cancer and In Life.* She now heads the Deanna Favre HOPE Foundation, whose mission is to provide assistance to women who are underserved or underinsured in their battle against breast cancer. Does having a wife who inspires hope make you a better quarterback? Not sure. But she certainly helps make you a better person.

Tough Guy

In the March 2004 issue of *Men's Journal*, Favre was chosen as the No. 1 "Toughest Guy in America" on the basis of his "fearlessness, perseverance, a willingness to take risk, a tolerance for pain and even a dash of modesty."

During his NFL-record 253 consecutive games started streak, Favre has played through a first-degree separation of his left shoulder (courtesy of a Reggie White hit), a severely bruised left hip, a severely sprained left ankle, tendonitis in his right elbow and a sprained lateral collateral ligament in his left knee. In 2003, against the St. Louis Rams, he broke his right thumb. Outfitted with a makeshift protective cap that made holding the ball difficult, Favre played the last

two months of the season in constant pain. Yet he still managed to finish the year with 32 touchdown passes and a quarterback rating over 90.

Pain, of course, is relative. You hit your thumb hard with a hammer and it hurts like a son of a gun. But when something happens to an NFL player during a game — a game you're watching from the comfort of your couch — it doesn't seem so bad. Let's face it: the distance from couch to field clouds everything. That's why we think players should be able to shake it off, ice it down, or shoot it up. Something. Anything. As long as they can get back on the field to play before you get back from the kitchen with more potato chips.

Of course, it doesn't work that way.

Willie Davis, the Packers Hall of Fame defensive end, didn't miss a game from 1960 through 1969. He knows a little something about playing through pain.

"If they were looking for a symbol for toughness in the dictionary they'd get Brett Favre," Davis said. "He is one of the gutsiest, toughest quarterbacks this league has ever seen. Those of us who watch him probably don't truly appreciate that he's played with pain, and played at times when lesser quarterbacks wouldn't have tried it."

The Big Hurt

Among the final pictures Deanna pulls from an album is one of Brett in his first football uniform. It's Christmas and he's a little more than a year old. His dad sits cross-legged on the floor, tucking the jersey into his son's pants. It's a simple, touching scene, made even more so because you know what is to become of the boy. And of the man.

The closest Brett Favre ever came to missing a football game in Green Bay was Dec. 23, 2003. No one would have blamed him if he had. He didn't have a dislocated shoulder or a sprained knee. Far worse: a broken heart.

The day before the Packers were to play the Raiders in Oakland on Monday Night Football, Favre's dad died of a massive heart attack while driving on a road near his home in Mississippi.

A mere 26 hours later, Favre not only played but he had the best statistical game of his career – 399 passing yards, four touchdowns, no interceptions. The Packers won 41-7, and a national television audience choked back tears.

The touchdowns and championships and awards help to give perspective to a career. Numbers don't lie. They just don't tell the whole story. Is Brett Favre the greatest quarterback of all time? The numbers sure make a strong argument. It's the man, however, who makes an even stronger one.

> *The measure of a man will never be in numbers, but rather in how he made life richer for others. For that reason, Favre stands taller than most.*

PHOTO COURTESY STEVE JACOBSON

As if they were on a playground, Favre hoists wide receiver Donald Driver onto his shoulders after the two combined for a touchdown against the San Francisco 49ers December 10, 2006.

BRIAN BAHR/GETTY IMAGES

Forever Young

Once Thought Long Lost, Brett Gave Us Something Magical — A Second Childhood

BY JOEL DRESANG

When I became a dad, a colleague clapped me on the back and told me that parenthood gives us a second childhood—from a different perspective. That is why I'm grateful to Brett Favre.

I grew up in the shadow of Title Town in a time known as the Glory Years. The pantheon of my heroes included Ray Nitschke, Jerry Kramer and Jim Taylor. All three were rookies in 1958, the year I was born, the season that Green Bay won one game and lost ten, including two humiliations to the Baltimore Colts and the Chicago Bears in which the combined score was 7 to 117.

The next year, Coach Vince Lombardi arrived, elevating those players, that team, the city of Green Bay, and impressionable boys in neighborhoods like mine. In three years, Lombardi's Packers yielded as many victories as his predecessors had accumulated in the seven previous seasons. Hardened players such as Forrest Gregg, Willie Davis, Henry Jordan, Jim Ringo and Paul Hornung toiled as teammates to accomplish championships, and in the process achieved personal status as some of the greatest players ever.

Every kid I knew followed the Packers, memorized their jersey numbers, sought their autographs at sports shows and restaurant openings. I learned to type by making copies of the Packers rosters. I practiced math by compiling game statistics from the evening newspaper. I studied the human form by sketching their pictures, including a poster of Davis I drew on a long section from a roll of scrap paper my father brought home from his job at the local paper mill.

Through these players, we witnessed the rewards of discipline and practice, of perseverance and camaraderie—traits we later would observe in and which would endear us to Favre. And, as we later would see with Favre, the most impressive laurels of those Packers

Favre reminded us that perseverance pays off, as it did for the Packers in a 28-24 playoff victory over the Detroit Lions on January 8, 1994. Favre threw the game-winning touchdown pass with less than a minute left in the game.

VERNON BIEVER/NFL/GETTY IMAGES

Legendary coach Vince Lombardi (center) and the Packers coaching staff in 1962. From left, Phil Bengtson, Tom Fears, Bill Austin, Lombardi, Red Cochran, Norb Hecker and Dick Voris.

of our youth were not the trophies or the rings but the smiles—mud-caked, frostbit, gap-toothed confirmations that winning was worth the effort.

Those players taught us that teamwork trumps talent. Without teamwork, Hornung, though he was a Heisman Trophy winner at Notre Dame, was a loser at football. With teamwork, Bart Starr, drafted in the 17th round, was a two-time Super Bowl MVP. And for the ignominious linemen—where they stuck us kids with slow feet and hard hands—teamwork propelled guys like Davis, Ringo, Gregg and Jordan into the Hall of Fame.

The Packers of my youth weren't glamorous, like TV stars, or adventurous, like astronauts. But unlike grownups engaged in more sober pursuits, we could imagine these Packers as kids. And as kids, we could imagine ourselves as Packers. We considered little difference between the football we played in our back yards and the combat they waged on Sundays.

We smelled the same sweet dewy grass, spat the same pungent mix of sweat and blood from our mouths, heard the same jarring crunch of bones as our bodies collided. The touchdown passes we heaved counted for as many points as any scoring strike from Starr to Max McGee or Boyd Dowler. The interceptions we snagged caused the same swing of momentum as any ball picked off by Willie Wood or Herb Adderley.

Had we been born a couple decades earlier, GIs might have been our collective heroes. But for post-war baby boomers, the Packers provided a green-and-gold buffer between the staid generation of our parents and the coming countercultural upheaval punctuated by riots, assassinations and conflict.

As we matured, we realized that our neighborhood football only nominally resembled the professional trade of our idols. The Packers prepared me better for typing and math than for the rigors of organized sports. In high school, I languished as a reserve offensive lineman on the junior varsity team. Then one day the head coach, who also was the geometry teacher, took me aside to say that he had a spot for me on varsity—as statistician.

College and career pursuits carried me away from northeastern Wisconsin. The farther I moved, the more difficulty I had following the team. But I always found Packer fans. And the Glory Years—the nostalgia and the trivia—bonded us.

In the 13 years between when I left my childhood home and moved back to Wisconsin to get married, the Packers had just two winning seasons, including their 5-3-1 record during the 1982 players strike.

Bart Starr was a 17th round pick of the Packers in 1956. He led the Packers to five NFL championships in the 1960s, including the first two Super Bowls.

Ray Nitschke came to the Packers as a fullback from the University of Illinois in 1958. Fifteen seasons later he retired as one of the fiercest middle linebackers to have ever played the game.

My wife was pregnant with our first child when Favre started as a Packer in 1992. Just as children jog memories of the joys and limitations of our own youth, so Favre harkened back to those Packers of the Glory Years.

He was cut from the same cloth, a throwback, a workingman's player, the consummate competitor, a tough guy. He flashed the impetuosity of McGee and Hornung but also the cleverness of Starr and the intuition of Nitschke. His ability and success made him a three-time National Football League MVP. But his durability, determination and demeanor put him in the same league as the Packers I had deified.

Sure, he revived winning traditions. But as with the Packers of old, Favre's most enduring attribute was his give-it-all gutsiness. Hawg Hanner played just 10 days after an appendectomy in 1961. Taylor overcame a gashed tongue and seven stitches in his elbow to power the Packers to victory in the 1962 title game. Kramer recovered to play after numerous surgeries, including lifesaving emergency removal of wooden splinters from his abdomen.

But not even those Packers prepared us for the breathtaking injuries, drug addiction and personal suffering that Favre played through on his way to the record books. His consecutive games streak of 253 testifies that Favre was the ultimate gamer.

Over time, life teaches us that heroes have flaws and that the constant pursuit of perfection and consistency can be more valuable than actually attaining them. Watching the boyish Favre through my grownup glasses, I have deeper appreciation for the Packers of my youth.

And again, the hard times and high honors pale in the glare of Favre's winning smile, his adolescent playfulness, his jubilant fireman's carries of touchdown receivers, his arms thrust skyward to signal another score.

Outside our bedrooms is a gallery of family photographs—immigrant great-grandparents, our parents in their youth, our grandparents holding babies, a timeline of portraits and snapshots of our daughters. The only frame that

Favre restored hope and pride among the long-suffering Packer faithful. The fact that he had a lot of fun while doing it made his career that much more rewarding for all.

doesn't include a blood relative is an autographed photo that Nitschke sent me when I was in grade school. In faded red careful penmanship, it says: "To a friend, Joel Dresang, May you always have the very best. Hit 'Em Hard, Ray Nitschke."

Nitschke had replied to my schoolboy plea for career advice on how to become a middle linebacker. I have kept it as a souvenir of my youthful ambitions and those heady days of World Championships forged from dedicated teamwork. Forever, I'll be impressed by how seriously he took my silly request and how thoughtfully he responded. It reminds me how far a simple kindness can go. And though I'm resigned to never play in the NFL, I still want to be Ray Nitschke.

On the wall across from Nitschke and my family is a photograph of Favre. It's from Favre's first full season as starting quarterback, the Packers' 75th anniversary.

Favre has just thrown a screen pass that a Dallas Cowboys defender has batted back. Favre's eyes are frozen on the ball, which is suspended in the air between him and the defensive lineman. Favre is off balance, midway through his follow-through. Still, you sense from the look in his eyes that he is figuring out how to keep that ball in play and make something happen.

Favre restored a can-do attitude among the Packers faithful. Lest we get greedy and expect too much, long-time fans should remember that we are long-suffering fans. Regardless of whether the team's fortunes revert to the humbling times between Lombardi and Favre, this latest taste of glory and titles shall live on.

Not only did Favre bring back pride to our little piece of the planet. He contributed another constellation to the heavens over Lambeau Field.

Joel Dresang is an award-winning journalist with the *Milwaukee Journal-Sentinel* and has been nominated for a regional Emmy for his work on Public Television.

By the time he was a senior, Favre was clearly the leader of the Golden Eagles. He completed 613 of 1,169 passes in 42 college games for 7,695 yards and 52 TDs.

A Legend Takes Shape

From Obscurity to Heisman Candidate at Southern Miss

BY CHUCK BENNETT

It's hard to believe, but Brett Favre was once tossed aside by some of the biggest college football programs in the South.

Some said he was too slow, while others were looking at him to play defensive back.

It's an amazing story how Favre ended up at the University of Southern Mississippi. Hang on, because like Favre's National Football League career, this ride through the courting of Favre by colleges and his years at USM was plenty wild.

The Recruiting War

Favre's high school was not necessarily one that makes high school football junkies and college recruiters swoon. Playing for his father, Irvin Favre, Brett never put up numbers that drew a lot of notice.

You never heard the words "blue chip" or "five star" associated with the name Brett Favre. College recruiters weren't exactly flattering either.

Irv, a former Southern Miss baseball pitcher in the late 1960s, remembered it well.

"In my coaching career, I've always tried to get my players some attention from recruiters. I have even tried to help kids from schools we played against," said the elder Favre. "When recruiters came through, I told them that Brett could help them. LSU was interested for a while, but they said he was a step slow.

"Florida came in, but they were looking for more of an option quarterback. Brett is not a great runner, but he can run the option. Mississippi State was interested too, but they backed away too."

LSU, Florida, Mississippi State and Mississippi all showed some interest, but none courted Favre.

On one hand, Irv might have been guilty of underexposing his son. The coach was known for his tough, hard-nosed teams at Hancock North Central. His teams annually turned out 1,000-yard rushers.

Brett ran the wishbone for his first two high school seasons and continued handing the ball to backs heading into his senior season.

As the college recruiters began backing away, one team and one coach stood ready to add Brett to their squad – Southern Miss. At the time the Golden Eagles were coached by Jim Carmody. Carmody and his staff weren't dying to add another quarterback to their roster.

Heading into the spring, Carmody had three able quarterbacks in Ailrick Young, Simmie Carter and David Forbes. Two other high school quarterbacks had already verbally cast their lot with the Eagles.

Assistant coach Mark McHale was assigned to recruit the Mississippi Gulf Coast. It was McHale who was credited in "finding" Favre and leading him to Southern Miss. McHale saw something special in Favre and watched his prep career with great interest.

But it wasn't easy for McHale to even get Carmody to watch Favre play. Carmody was simply not interested in signing a quarterback, let alone one that couldn't throw much. McHale tells a great recruiting story eventually paid great dividends for the Eagles.

As McHale's relationship with Irv Favre became more comfortable, McHale asked him to put on a show during Hancock's last home game. That meant Brett was going to have to put the ball in the air.

"Irvin would only throw the ball four or five times per game," said McHale, who worked on the staff at Marshall for five years before recently taking a job with Bobby Bowden at Florida State. "I said, Irvin, I have the head coach coming to see Brett. He thinks we are looking at Brett as a defensive back. I need you to let Brett throw the ball and show what he can do."

McHale told Southern Miss staff that Favre had a great future playing defensive back at the Division I level. As legend has it, with McHale and Carmody in the stands, Irv really let Brett loose and Brett attempted six passes that night.

Regardless, Southern Miss continued to stay in touch with the Favres and, late into the recruiting year, offered Brett a football scholarship. Only Division II power Delta State had a counter offer.

"When Southern Miss signed me, it was the greatest moment of my life," says Brett. "A few bigger schools showed interest for a while. But Southern Miss really hung in there, particularly coach McHale. I guess some people might have considered me a long shot, but I was just happy to get an opportunity."

"The story of how Brett was recruited is a great one," says former Southern Miss head coach Curley Hallman, who replaced Carmody after Favre's freshman year. "Here's a kid from a small school that didn't throw much, and now he's one of the best quarterbacks in the country. It just shows that you can't always judge a player in physical talent alone."

Playing Time

Favre reported to the Hattiesburg, Miss., campus in early August, 1987. In the beginning, he garnered little attention from the coaches and players.

"The freshman came into camp a few days early," says former Southern Miss receiver Chris McGee. "Brett was not the most highly regarded quarterback to come to camp; Michael Jackson was. Jackson was the next Reggie Collier."

Favre wasn't even on the depth chart when junior Ailrick Young earned the starting role in the spring. He was followed on the depth charts by Simmie Carter and David Forbes.

"When I first came here, I was depressed," Favre said. "I sat up in the dorm with nothing to look forward to except practice in the morning and afternoon. You sit there and you think about the fact that you were a starter in high school and all of a sudden you're a nobody. It really gets you down."

Early in the preseason, Forbes went down with a knee injury and the Southern Miss coaching staff elevated Jackson to third-string status. Even being third-string was important, because the Southern Miss staff always traveled with three quarterbacks. Shortly after Jackson moved into the role, he, too, was hit with an injury. Favre was put into the third slot.

"I remember looking at the other quarterbacks. I used to envy Ailrick (Young) and David (Forbes). They were somebody," Favre said. "The coaches looked up to them, the rest of the players looked up to them. And I was back there throwing for the scout team."

Favre began turning heads during two-a-day practices and the potential that coach McHale saw in Brett began to show itself to the rest of the Southern Miss coaching staff and players.

"He split my hands open a couple times during practice," said McGee. "We used to have a sit route where the receiver runs a 5 to 7-yard route and sits, the quarterback takes a four-step drop and hits you. The first time Brett got into the rotation to work with the receivers, he threw the ball and Darryl Tillman moved out of the way. I said, 'Tillman, What are you doing?' He said, 'I thought he was throwing the ball down the field.'"

McGee would get a laugh at the expense of fellow receiver Tillman, but the laughter quickly turned to amazement as McGee lined up in the same passing drill.

"In that same practice, I ran the same route and he threw the ball to me," said McGee, who would later be on the receiving end of the first career touchdown pass that Favre would toss in Hattiesburg. "Not 10 yards from me, he threw the ball as hard as he could. He did not have any touch. I caught the ball and threw it back to him.

"You have to realize I was a senior offensive captain and he was just a 17-year-old kid. I said, 'What the heck are you trying to do?' I think I earned his respect that day because I caught the ball. He and I became friends that year."

As preseason practice wrapped up, the Golden Eagles prepped for an opening season game at Alabama. The Crimson Tide was had a new new coach in Bill Curry. Alabama had often dominated Southern

ALLEN STEELE//GETTY IMAGES

Southern Mississippi Career Stats

Year	GP	Att	Cmp	Yards	Comp%	Y/Att	Int	TD
1987	10	194	79	1,264	.407	6.5	13	15
1988	11	319	178	2,271	.558	7.1	5	16
1989	11	381	206	2,588	.541	6.8	10	14
1990	10	275	150	1,572	.545	5.7	6	7
Totals	42	1169	613	7,695	.524	6.6	34	52

Note: Totals do not include two Southern Miss Bowl Games

Miss and Favre's first game against the Tide was much the same.

The Southern Miss offense sputtered, mustering only 69 passing yards with three interceptions. The Eagles tried both Young and Carter at quarterback, neither impressed and the Eagles lost 38-6.

Returning to MM Roberts Stadium, the Eagles had a week layoff before heading into the Tulane game. Favre stayed No. 3 on the depth charts, but that did not keep him from having a little fun.

"The night before the Tulane game, we went with the team to see a movie. We were allowed to drive back then and on the way back we bought a case and half of beer," rememberd offensive lineman Chris Ryals, one of Favre's old roommates. "We were not expecting to play the next day. We each drank 18 beers. I remember it well; it was a great Friday night TV lineup – Johnny Carson and David Letterman. We both loved those shows. We sat around watching TV until 3 a.m."

Expecting to own a seat next to Ryals on the Golden Eagle bench, Favre and the rest of the rookies watched as the Southern Miss offense struggled once again. Down 16-10 to the Green Wave at home, the Southern Miss staff decided to put Favre into the game during the second possession of the second half.

His first touchdown strike (a 7-yard pass to McGee) put Southern Miss up 17-16. Another touchdown toss sealed the 31-24 win.

"Tulane also had a first-year coach," said McGee. "They had scouted us well against Alabama and they were shutting us down in the first half. Alrick and Simmie were terrible. In the third quarter they put in Favre and we changed our whole offense. We went from an option-based offense to throwing the ball. Tulane had eight, nine in the box and we started throwing.

"Tulane was not ready for Favre," McGee laughed.

To this day, no one is totally sure whose idea is was to insert Favre in the game; however, former Southern Miss head coach Jeff Bower remembers halftime of the Tulane game.

"Coach Carmody asked for recommendations," says Bower who was offensive coordinator at the time. "I told him we needed a spark, and that we needed to get Brett in there. I really felt he could get it done."

Carmody resigned under pressure following the season. The Eagles finished 6-5 with a quality win over SEC foe and in-state rival Mississippi State.

Favre played wild at times, relying on his big arm to try to win games. There was a four-interception performance against Florida State, a weak performance against Jackson State (3 of 7, 64 yards and one interception) and he was actually benched in the second half of the Mississippi State game.

Something happened, however, during the last two games of the year, when Favre went 33 of 59 for 527 yards and five touchdowns in games against East Carolina and Southwestern Louisiana.

"You knew you had something special (in Favre) after the Southwestern Louisiana game," said McGee. "We all said that Brett had his breakout game that night. I knew then that that boy was something special."

The Legend Grows

While Favre was blessed with a solid offensive line his freshman campaign, the team had a lot of question marks going into his sophomore year. First, there was new head coach Curley Hallman calling the shots.

"One thing I remember was working out with the offense," says former Southern Miss defensive standout John Brown. "The offensive line during Brett's second year was made up of former defensive lineman and guys just thrown together. I was playing tight end at the time.

"I was running a 'look in' and as I turned in, all I could hear was the wind coming off the ball. I was trying to get my hands on the ball and it was very difficult. Brett had no touch back then and we just tried to protect ourselves. Brett came out his second year to prove something, and he just threw the balls hard as he could."

Once again, Favre started the season slowly with just 121 yards passing in an opening win against Stephen F. Austin. The following week, he threw an interception on the second play of the game to former Florida State All-American Deion Sanders — one that Sanders returned for a score.

Favre began to settle down and threw three touchdowns in a win over Virginia Tech. The next week it was 300-plus yards and a win over East Carolina. His success continued with three touchdown passes against Tulane, another three against Southwestern Louisiana. By the end of the year, Favre had led his team to a 9-2 regular season with the only loses to Florida State and Auburn.

Favre is remembered by many team members for his down home nature and friendship with his offensive line.

"He hung out with the lineman," says Ryals, currently a network administrator for Hancock Bank. "Brett's freshman year he had five senior offensive linemen, he comes back the next year with five guys who never played a lick. I guess he knew he had to be friends with us and encourage us."

Brown also remembers Favre as one of the big boys.

"At Southern Miss, you could be a down-home guy and still be a superstar. He would go and eat with the offensive linemen all the time. I remember some of the guys like Chris Ryals and Chafin Marsh eating pickled pig feet with Favre. They always had a jar hidden under their bed," Brown laughs.

"Brett would go down and eat pickled pigs feet. Only the offensive lineman and Brett were allowed in their room to eat. Brett was always with his offensive line. I remember, while I was with the offensive line my first two years I was allowed to eat with them; then I transferred to defensive line. When I went back, they said no more pickled pig feet."

"We had a little fraternity with the linemen. Back then we were all friends," said Ryals. "There was so much loyalty to each other. Brett was one of us. We tried our hardest for him because we knew he was going to do his best for us. It was fun."

Favre led his squad to a berth in the Independence Bowl and a win over UTEP. He was named the Bowl's Offensive Player of the Game.

In all, Favre finished 1988 breaking several school records, including passing for 2,271 yards and 16 touchdowns.

Excitement and anticipation were alive and well as the Golden Eagles started the 1989 campaign. Heading into his junior season, Favre was viewed by many preseason publications as one of the top offensive players in the South.

FAVRE FACTS
from his days at Southern Miss

- Eugene Rowell caught Favre's first pass Sept. 19, 1987 vs. Tulane.
- Chris McGee caught Favre's first touchdown pass Sept. 19, 1987 vs. Tulane.
- Played for three head coaches (Jim Carmody, Curley Hallman and Jeff Bower). Bower coached the 1990 All-American Bowl when Hallman accepted the LSU job.
- His first roommate was 6-foot-8, 270-pounder Chris Ryals from Purvis, Miss.
- Ironically, two of the quarterbacks ahead of Favre in 1987 were later moved to different positions, both going on to play professionally; Simmie Carter played cornerback for the Birmingham Fire of the WLAF and Michael Jackson played receiver for Cleveland Browns and Baltimore Ravens of the NFL.
- Mark Montgomery caught the last touchdown of Favre's career on Dec. 28, 1990, at the All-American Bowl vs. North Carolina State.
- Jackson caught the last pass of Favre's career on Dec. 28, 1990, at the All-American Bowl vs. North Carolina State.
- Threw for a career-high 345 yards on Oct. 28, 1989 vs. Memphis State.
- Currently holds (or tied) nine Southern Miss season or career records.
- Holds the Southern Miss record with 7,695 career passing yards.
- Tied with former Southern Miss quarterback Lee Roberts with 52 career touchdown passes.
- Had 15 career 200-yard passing games.
- Had a school record five 300-yard passing games.
- Longest touchdown passes was an 80-yard bomb to Ron Baham on Sept. 30, 1989 vs. Texas A&M.
- Completed a career-best 26 passes on Nov. 25, 1989, vs. East Carolina.
- Played in four televised games, going 3-1 in those games.
- Played in front of 85,214, the most ever in his career in a win over Auburn on Nov. 10, 1990.
- Went 3-5 against nationally ranked opponents during his career.
- Named second team All-South Independent in 1990.
- His No. 4 is one of only two retired numbers at Southern Miss, the other being Ray Guy's 44.
- Named to the Southern Miss Legend's Club.
- Named to the Southern Miss Football Team of the Century.
- Inducted to the Southern Miss 'M' Club Hall of Fame on April 18, 1997.

The Kiln, Miss., native did not disappoint, leadingd the Golden Eagles to an opening season 30-26 win over No. 6. Florida State.

"It really disappoints me, but it does not surprise me," said FSU coach Bobby Bowden. "We had held Favre pretty well for two years in a row. I figured he was due."

It was Favre who engineered a 13-play, 58-yard drive late in the second half to secure the win and a jump into the national spotlight. It was Favre's first win over a nationally ranked team. Following the big victory, the Golden Eagles were ranked 18th by the Associated Press and the ESPN-Coaches Polls. It was the team's first ranking since December of 1981.

In addition, Favre was chosen UPI's Offensive Back of the Week for his 282-yard, two-touchdown performance.

The national spotlight quickly faded away as Southern Miss would drop its next four consecutive games to Mississippi State, Auburn, Texas Christian and Texas A&M.

The Eagles rebounded to win four of their last six games, but the streak was not good enough to prevent a losing season (5-6).

Once again, there were bright spots for Favre. He tossed for a school record 345 yards in a win over then Memphis State. He also threw for 303 yards against a tough Texas A&M squad and 300 vs. Alabama.

Heading into his senior season, Favre was gathering lots of attention, but nobody could have foreseen than it would be an accident that would put him into the national spotlight. In late July prior to the time they were to report to camp, Favre suffered several serious injuries as a result of a car wreck.

Favre was hospitalized at Forrest General Hospital in Hattiesburg. There was so much media attention that Favre was listed under an assumed name.

After a five-plus-day stay in the hospital, Favre was released. He spent much of the next few weeks trying to regain his strength. After failing to recover, Favre took himself back to the hospital, where doctors found that 30-plus inches of his intestines had died. More surgery was needed for the removal of the dead tissue.

With a game against Delta State just a week away, it looked like Favre may have been lost for the season. Second-team quarterback Jon Whitcomb replaced Favre and directed the Eagles to a 12-0 win in Hattiesburg.

With Favre again not expected to play, the Eagles traveled to Birmingham to take on Alabama. Against all odds, Favre recovered enough to take the field and engineer a 27-24 upset win over the 13th-ranked Crimson Tide. It was his second win over a nationally ranked team.

"When you play with a guy like Brett, you don't know how special he is because you are around him all the time," says Brown. "He was always joking around. When people talk about how tough he is, they really do not understand unless you have played with him. I remember before the Alabama game. Everyone was wondering when Brett was coming back. When he started back to practice, you could tell he was hurting. He must have lost 50 pounds from the surgery. It was remarkable. He had a drive that most people cannot understand. There is a reason he is so tough today."

Favre saved his best senior outing for a highly anticipated game against 15th-ranked Auburn. Favre threw for 207 yards and two touchdowns leading Southern Miss in the 13-12 upset.

He was definitely a big man on campus, but the attention never changed Favre — something that his former teammates remember well and still appreciate.

"It was an honor to him (the national attention), but it did not mean that much," says Ryals. "He never liked to do things to bring attention to himself. He did not have any 'Favre 4 Heisman' posters

Favre and head coach Jerry Glanville of the Falcons.

hanging in the dorm room. He knows he is just a common ol' Joe, doing his job like the rest of us."

Still, the Southern Miss coaching staff kept close tabs on Favre's practice and activities.

"I remember once during practice, I had beaten the offensive tackle on a passing drill. Brett was prime property, you did not touch Brett," said Brown. "You were not allowed in close proximity to him. I was sick of protecting the golden child. So, I hit him slightly, just to let him know I was still around. Well, just to let you know, I got jumped by a few coaches. My helmet was snatched off and thrown across the field."

The 8-3 regular-season finish propelled Southern Miss into its second bowl game of the Favre era. The Golden Eagles were invited to play North Carolina State in the All-American Bowl.

Once again, Favre did not disappoint. He threw for 341 yards and two touchdowns, but it was not quite enough as North Carolina State pulled off a 31-27 victory.

The two big wins over Auburn and Alabama promoted Hallman's stature in the coaching ranks and he was named head coach at Louisiana State University.

Hallman had accepted the job just two weeks prior to Southern Miss playing N.C. State.

NFL, Here I Come

For his college career, Favre played in 42 games and threw for a school record 7,695 yards and 52 touchdowns.

For his efforts, he was selected to play in the Senior Bowl and the East-West Shrine Game. He fared well in both games and continued to prep for his upcoming NFL career. He was still the same low-key "good old boy" he had always been, even after with a legendary college career behind him.

"Giant killer was accurate back then, now there is so much parity," said Brown. "We had monumental wins for Southern Miss. Just having Brett as a QB, you were guaranteed a touchdown or two. He inspired the defense. You were always in the game with Brett."

Despite his accolades at Southern Miss, NFL teams were still a little unsure about Favre. He had played only four games on TV, with only one of those games (1990 All-American Bowl) being played under the national spotlight.

Favre eventually waited for the second round before the Atlanta Falcons grabbed him with the 33rd overall pick of the 1991 NFL Draft. Ironically, both Michael Jackson (sixth round, Cleveland Browns) and Simmie Carter (seventh round, New York Giants), two quarterbacks whom Favre had replaced, were both taken in the same NFL Draft.

From there, well, you know the rest. The glorious college career was just the start of something big. As beloved as Favre was in Hattiesburg, his popularity there would pale in comparison to the aclaim and admiration he would receive in the NFL.

Once Favre got into pro football, his days as an unknown gunslinger from little Kiln, Miss., were over.

The Brett I Knew

A Behind-The-Scene View of a
Young Quarterback Coming Of Age

BY CHUCK BENNETT

The first time I heard the name Brett Favre was in February, 1986. It was signing day at Southern Miss and I was working as the assistant sports information director for the athletic department.

While I was always excited around signing day, quite frankly, we really did not do any flips when we had to write up the Brett Favre bio to release to the media attending the signing day functions.

Signing Day at Southern Miss was not like the collegiate football powerhouses. As much as I can remember, we never signed any All-Americans at Southern Miss.

Not much attention was paid to the players we signed, we never had a class rated in the Top 20; so Favre was pretty much like the other guys, not to get excited about.

Again, when August rolled around, we were anxious about the start of a new season; however, the expectations were not very high.

Heading into the 1987 season, we were coming off a 6-5 year with a head coach (Jim Carmody) on the hot seat. Couple that with a schedule that included Alabama, Texas A&M, Florida State and Mississippi State and, well you get the picture.

Favre was a breath of fresh air when he led the Golden Eagles to a 31-24 victory over Tulane. I still remember that game. No fans or media types really knew much about Brett, heck most of the athletic staff was unaware of the guy.

Brett did bring his cheering section. Fans often recall his faithful family members and their gold "Favre" T-shirts. The entire stands fell to a complete hush as Brett dropped back and threw the ball a mile. Of course, the pass went incomplete but the "wow factor" had kicked in.

You know how fans can be, they were pumped. Favre's two touchdown passes were the key to us winning the Tulane game and it is still remembered as one of Brett's most memorable games.

Still, Brett played up and down his freshman year and he really stayed under the radar for the most part. Heck, in his last home game of the year, only 11,023 turned out to watch and that is being kind.

Most of the media and fan attention toward the end of the season was thrown upon the coaching situation at Southern Miss. Shortly following the season, Carmody was let go and then Athletic Director Bill McLellan brought in Curley Hallman from Texas A&M.

As preseason 1988 rolled around, there was optimism in the air, mostly because of the new coaching staff. Sure, Brett was a returning starter. However, he had five new offensive linemen, including at least one freshman.

Brett played real well his sophomore season. Personally, I think it was his best year at Southern Miss, throwing for 16 touchdowns and only five interceptions. He led the team to a 10-2 record that year.

Consider this, in 1988 Southern Miss played only four games in Hattiesburg. The only two loses that season were to Florida State and Auburn, both nationally ranked teams at the time.

I remember Brett having a huge cheering section. His mom and dad and every cousin, nephew, niece and neighbor showed up in Hattiesburg to support Brett. They would all wear match shirts saying stuff like "Brett Favre's Mom," "Brett Favre's Aunt" and so forth. They were a great support group.

Following our 9-2 regular season, we were invited to play in the Independence Bowl. You can go ahead and laugh now, but back then it was a huge deal.

Southern Miss had not played in a Bowl Game since 1981 when coach Bobby Collins led a 9-1-1 team into the Tangerine Bowl. Also consider that Brett Favre had never played on television. That's right; the 1988 Independence Bowl vs. UTEP was the first time a national audience had the chance to see Favre.

I remember the Independence Bowl well. Prior to game day, the UTEP players came up with a rap song degrading Southern Miss. This really ticked off Favre and the rest of the team. Brett liked to shy away from the limelight but don't ever try to show him up.

Defensive back/punt return specialist James Henry scored two touchdowns, while Brett threw for another as Southern Miss won a 38-18 game over UTEP. It was just the second-ever bowl victory in Southern Miss football history.

As we were preparing for spring football McLellan called his athletic staff together one Friday afternoon. Coach Mac (that's what we liked to call him) went on to tell us that Favre and Deanna were about to be parents. McLellan swore us to secrecy, we were to be prepared as a media relations staff but this was to never get out.

I still remember the following Sunday's newspaper headlines screamed Favre was going to be a father. We got a kick out of it. While the Southern Miss staff was trying to keep everything hush-hush, Bonita Favre was so excited she was out telling everyone she could.

And that's what the Favres were like. They were great family people, still are today. Brett's parents were so excited about Brittany's arrival.

All during his sophomore season and into his junior year, I would meet from time to time with Irvin Favre. Irvin was always wanting to get Brett more press, but Brett never really cared much about all the publicly.

I still remember walking into Coach Mac's office and saying I wanted $10,000 to do a Brett Favre 4 Heisman Campaign. Coach Mac laughed and then screamed at me when he realized I was serious.

We did not have a bunch of extra money lying around at Southern Miss, however, he was willing to allow me to go into this venture, but we had to come up with the extra revenue.

When I called Irvin that night, he was fired up. We both knew that the Heisman Trophy was not in reach for a player at Southern Miss, we both were just dying for some publicity – for both Brett and Southern Miss athletics.

The local Miller Beer distributor agreed to pony up a little cash and I went ahead with the plans. I don't really remember Brett being that excited, as I said before I remember him as one who liked to shy away from all the extra publicity.

That summer leading up to the start of the 1989 season I would send out news and notes about Favre. We got a lot of local and even statewide press, but it was the national attention we were craving.

Once again, you must stop and realize that Southern Miss was not on television. We played as an independent, and our teams took beatings on the road to the likes of Alabama, Auburn, Florida State, Penn State, etc. just so we could make our athletic department budget.

As the opening game against Florida State drew near, the publicity was working. I still have the clippings from several national newspapers and magazines as Favre's name was repeated again and again; and then it happened.

In a game scheduled for Hattiesburg (coach Mac sold the game to Jacksonville, Fla.) Brett Favre and Co. whipped number six ranked Florida State 30-26. Immediately, the phones rang off the hook. I was back in Hattiesburg working the offices even before the team had arrived home.

To me, this was a big step forward in the evolution of Southern Miss into a "player" in college football.

First, the game was televised by WTBS; only Favre's second time to play on TV. Second, the game vaulted us into the top 20.

Favre shocked the college football world by leading the Southern Mississippi Golden Eagles past Florida State 30-26, September 2, 1989, at Roberts Stadium in Hattiesburg, Mississippi.

While some readers may shrug this off, once again consider that Southern Miss had never been ranked in the ESPN Top 20 poll and prior the last AP ranking was on Dec. 1, 1981.

In addition, a CNN sports anchor held up one of our Favre 4 Heisman bumper stickers on national TV that night and said something like, "Here's the best player you have never hear of."

It was all coming together.

Then I received the phone call that media relation types love to receive, *The Sporting News'* national syndicated collegiate football radio show was highlighting five players the following week, one each day Monday through Friday and Favre was chosen for Tuesday.

I worked closely with Brett Sunday and Monday prepping him for his national radio interview. I guess I should have known better, anyway, come Tuesday Brett is a no-show for the interview.

He went out with a few buddies and blew off the interview. Boy, was I mad. I called Irvin and complained. We just blew the best chance to get that publicity, but it was about to get worse.

The next week, riding a wave of excitement, 34,189 – then the largest crowd ever at Hattiesburg's MM Roberts Stadium – showed up to watch the Golden Eagles host Mississippi State.

We were better than State that year, but as luck would have it, with former coach Carmody serving as State's defensive coordinator; State went on to a 26-23 victory.

It was tough to swallow. We had so much national attention following the FSU win, Southern Miss fans just love to hate State anyway and Carmody was carried off on the players shoulder to boot.

Could it get any worse? Sure, we went on to lose the next three consecutive games to start the season 1-4. It got so bad that the crowds dwindled down to a mere 11,189 at the East Carolina game. What once looked like a promising season turned out to be a below average 5-6 year at Southern Miss.

For his part, Favre had a decent season, but how many 5-6 quarterbacks get votes for All-Conference let alone any high awards? Brett threw for a career best 2,563 yards and 14 touchdowns.

For the most part, Brett just enjoyed playing. In a recent conversation I had with his former roommate, Chris Ryals, he confirmed what I remembered.

All during the season, Brett would avoid the phones calls from the media relations department when he could. In fact, he would have teammates answer his phone and tell the SID that he was out to class.

In July 1990, the well documented Favre car accident occurred putting a major hold on all of the preseason publicity we'd worked so hard to get.

I remember calling the local hospital to talk with Brett's family when the hospital spokesman told me he could not confirm whether or not Brett was in the hospital. At times things looked so bad that many wondered whether Favre would ever play again.

I remember following the accident, coach Hallman kept things very close, we were not to give out much information regarding Favre and his playing status.

That opening game in 1990 was odd. We beat Delta State by a slim 12-0 margin, but it was not the win that all the beat writers wanted to talk about, it was Favre.

I remember Brett doing his best to avoid all the accident talk. Heading into the Alabama game, not even his teammates knew whether or not he would play. Just his suiting up by itself inspired his squad to upset nationally ranked Alabama 27-24.

Brett led Southern Miss to an 8-3 regular season record and a berth in the All-American Bowl. Once again, Favre would be the publicity machine during his senior season. Wins over Alabama and Auburn actually propelled Hallman to accept the Louisiana State University job in December of 1990.

Brett participated in the Senior Bowl and East-West Shrine Game

Favre went from an unknown recruit to one of the best players in the nation at Southern Miss.

following his senior season. Like most athletes of his level, he spent most of his time preparing for the draft, although I remember him golfing most of the time.

I do remember Brett being ticked off when Seattle selected Dan McGwire as the first quarterback in the 1991 NFL Draft, while Oakland followed by drafting Todd Marinovich. Favre was actually the third QB taken in that draft.

Today, Brett and his family are very much still a part of the Southern Miss and Hattiesburg community. Unlike many of today's star athletes, Brett is different. He still cuts his own grass and drives his kids to school.

Of all the star athletes that Southern Miss has produced, Favre will always stand out as someone special. Despite actively staying out of the limelight, he brought national attention to a mid-major football school that today is often referred to as Brett Favre's school.

Editor's note: This is a first-person account of the author's work behind the scenes as the University of Mississippi's assistant sports information director.

Favre's first touchdown pass in Lambeau Field went to Sterling Sharpe in 1992. His last TD pass during the regular season was to Bubba Franks on December 30, 2007.

MORRY GASH/AP PHOTO

The Lord of Lambeau

No Quarterback Ruled the Frozen Tundra Like Favre

BY ERIC GOSKA

Cincinnati Bengals defensive tackle Doug Wilkinson couldn't get his left arm up in time to block the throw. Back judge Tony Corrente ducked near the 10-yard line so his head wouldn't be taken off by the pigskin missile that whizzed overhead. Free safety Darryl Williams lunged in a futile attempt to disrupt the play, and strong safety Bracey Walker crossed in front of the receiver a sliver of a second after Packers wide receiver Mark Ingram welcomed the ball into his hands.

Brett Favre had just thrown another touchdown pass at Lambeau Field.

For 16 years, Favre unloaded lethal lasers like the one against the Bengals in 1995. From 1992 through 2007, the Mississippi native threw 209 touchdown passes in 118 regular-season games at Lambeau. The 209 touchdown passes at Lambeau is an NFL record for most scoring throws at one venue.

Given the length of his career and his uncanny knack for finding open receivers, it's no surprise that the freewheeling quarterback threw far more touchdown passes at Lambeau Field than any other passer. But what might give one pause is the fact that Favre threw more touchdown passes in that venue than all other Packers passers combined.

Lambeau Field, then called New City Stadium, opened in 1957. In the 51 years the facility has been in operation, 21 Packers have thrown a total of 380 touchdown passes there during the regular season. The 20 Green Bay passers not named Favre accounted for 171 of those scores, or 38 short of the quarterback who repeatedly put the TD in Tundra.

The resumes of some of those 20 players were impressive. Bart Starr won five NFL champions during the 1960s and is in the Pro Football Hall of Fame. Two decades later, Lynn Dickey was the trigger man on some of the greatest Packers offenses ever. In 1989, Don Majkowski piloted a team that came from behind to win seven times and set an NFL record with four 1-point wins.

All told, Starr threw 40 scoring strikes at Lambeau Field; Dickey authored 39; and Majkowski 18. The trio's numbers pale next to those of Favre, though it must be pointed out that the three did not play eight games a year at Lambeau Field as Favre did beginning in 1995. Up to that point, the Packers split their regular season games between Green Bay and Milwaukee.

Still, 148 regular-season games had been played at the stadium before Favre first ducked under center for Green Bay in 1992. In 30 fewer games, Favre outdid all his predecessors combined to become No. 1 at the stadium named in honor of Curly Lambeau.

Because of the sheer volume of Favre's work, many of his touchdowns faded from memory as he continued his assault on the record book. Some of his throws, however, remain as memorable today as when they first occurred. The 13-yard bullet that the Bengals' Walker and Williams were helpless to defend triggered 21 unanswered points in a 24-10 victory on Dec. 3, 1995. Three years earlier, Favre teamed with Kitrick Taylor on a 35-yard score that beat the Bengals 24-23 and delivered Mike Holmgren's first win as coach. Against the Giants in 2004, Favre suffered a concussion, sat out two plays, and then returned to launch a 28-yard touchdown toss to Javon Walker on fourth down. How amazing was that touchdown pass? Doctors later informed coach Mike Sherman that his quarterback should not have left the bench.

Favre's sensational throw to Taylor in 1992 was not his first touchdown pass. His first as both a pro and at Lambeau Field was a 5-yarder to wide receiver Sterling Sharpe earlier in that game. His last (during the regular season) occurred 15 years later when he flipped a 4-yarder to tight end Bubba Franks on Dec. 30, 2007.

During the 16 years that Favre outperformed all other Packers passers, he also hummed along at a pace far better than the competition. In the 118 games in which he participated, opposing quarterbacks threw 138 touchdown passes, or 71 fewer than the Iron Man himself.

Favre was at his peak from 1995 through 1997 when he fired 23, 19 and 19 touchdown passes, respectively, at Lambeau Field. Those 61 scoring throws were offset by just 18 interceptions as the Packers fashioned a 23-1 home record (a .958 winning percentage) during that span.

During those three years, Favre's mastery of the air ensured a Packers receiver reached the end zone about once in every 13 throws. His composite passer rating for those 24 games was a lofty 101.1. Not surprisingly, he was named league MVP in each of those seasons.

Six times he tallied four or more touchdown tosses during that incredible run and twice he had games of five touchdowns or more. The first occurred on Nov. 12, 1995, when he overcame a severely sprained ankle to hook up twice with wide receiver Robert Brooks and running back Edgar Bennett and once with running back Dorsey Levens as Green Bay toppled the Bears 35-28. On Sept. 21, 1997, he riddled the Vikings' secondary with touchdown passes to wideouts Brooks, Antonio Freeman (twice) and Terry Mickens and tight end Mark Chmura in a 38-32 victory.

Of course, Favre wouldn't have been as proficient had the Packers not been blessed with some solid receivers. Thirty-four players caught at least one touchdown pass from Favre at Lambeau Field. Twenty-eight will be able to tell their grandchildren they did it more than once.

> *It's no surprise that Favre threw far more touchdown passes at Lambeau Field than any other passer. What is amazing is the fact that he threw more touchdowns in Lambeau than all other Packers passers combined.*

AL BELLO /ALLSPORT/GETTY IMAGES

Favre filled the Lambeau air with touchdown passes. His 209 TDs are an NFL record for most in one venue. Derrick Mayes (80) caught five TD passes from Favre from 1996-1998.

PUTTING THE TD IN TUNDRA

The 21 Packers players who threw a touchdown pass during the regular season at Lambeau Field from 1957 through 2007.

TDs	Player	Years Played
209	Brett Favre	1992-2007
40	Bart Starr	1956-71
39	Lynn Dickey	1976-77, 1979-85
18	Don Majkowski	1987-92
9	David Whitehurst	1977-83
8	Lamar McHan	1959-60
8	Don Horn	1967-70
8	Scott Hunter	1971-73
8	Randy Wright	1984-88
7	Babe Parilli	1957-58
5	Zeke Bratkowski	1963-68, 1971
3	John Roach	1961-63
3	Jim Zorn	1985
3	Anthony Dilweg	1989-90
3	Mike Tomczak	1991
2	John Hadl	1974-75
2	Willard Harrell	1975-77
2	Alan Risher	1987
1	Jim Del Gaizo	1973
1	Jack Concannon	1974
1	Carlos Brown	1975-76

Favre's fab five at the fabled field—and the only players to figure in on more than 10 scores—were Freeman (36 touchdown receptions), Brooks (17), Franks (16), Sharpe (14) and Donald Driver (13). Freeman and Favre set the Lambeau standard when they collaborated on 11 touchdown throws in 1998 alone.

As the 1990s gave way to a new decade, Favre's production slowed some. Aside from 2004 (16 touchdown passes), the aging quarterback never managed more than 15 scoring throws at Lambeau from 1999 through 2007. In 2006, his first year under coach Mike McCarthy, Favre threw just six touchdown passes at home ending a string of 12 straight seasons in which he compiled at least 10.

Fortunately, Favre returned for one more go-round after that low point. With a young, but talented, group of receivers that included rookie James Jones and second-year wideout Greg Jennings, Favre fired 14 touchdown passes in 2007 in front of hometown fans during a resurgent 13-3 season.

In his last regular-season game at Lambeau, Favre completed 9 of 11 attempts for 99 yards and two scores. His final completion went to Franks for a touchdown early in the second quarter that gave the Packers a 21-3 lead as they went on to rout the Lions 34-13 and reach the playoffs for the 11th times in 16 seasons with the most prolific touchdown maker in Lambeau Field history at the helm.

Eric Goska is a nationally recognized number-crunching guru of all things Packers. Goska has written a "by the numbers" column about the Packers since 1994. He has provided statistics for such books as *Favre: For the Record, Return to Glory: The Inside Story of the Green Bay Packers' Return to Prominence* and *Mudbaths and Bloodbaths.* He has also written two editions of *Green Bay Packers: A Measure of Greatness.*

A Passing Fancy

From Touchdown Passes to Career WIns, the Stats Say No. 4 is No. 1

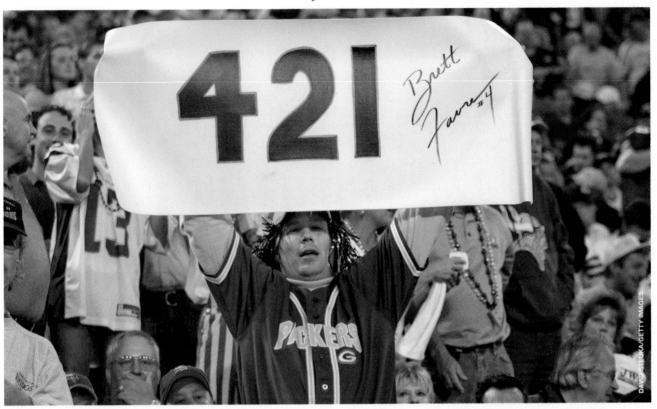

A fan of the Packers displays a sign after Brett Favre breaks the all-time touchdown passing record against the Vikings at the Hubert H. Humphrey Metrodome on September 30, 2007 in Minneapolis. The Packers beat the Vikings 23-16.

NFL ALL-TIME RECORDS

PASSING YARDAGE		PASSES ATTEMPTED		TOTAL PASSES COMPLETED		TOTAL TD PASSES		CAREER WINS AS A QB	
1) BRETT FAVRE	61,655	1) BRETT FAVRE	8,758	1) BRETT FAVRE	5,377	1) BRETT FAVRE	442	1) BRETT FAVRE	160
2) DAN MARINO	61,361	2) DAN MARINO	8,358	2) DAN MARINO	4,967	2) DAN MARINO	420	2) JOHN ELWAY	148
3) JOHN ELWAY	51,475	3) JOHN ELWAY	7,250	3) JOHN ELWAY	4,123	3) FRAN TARKENTON	342	3) DAN MARINO	147
4) WARREN MOON	49,325	4) WARREN MOON	6,823	4) WARREN MOON	3,988	4) PEYTON MANNING	306	4) FRAN TARKENTON	125
5) FRAN TARKENTON	47,003	5) DREW BLEDSOE	6,717	5) DREW BLEDSOE	3,839	5) JOHN ELWAY	300	5) JOHNNY UNITAS	119
6) VINNY TESTAVERDE	46,233	6) VINNIE TESTAVERDE	6,701	6) VINNY TESTAVERDE	3,787	6) WARREN MOON	291		
7) DREW BLEDSOE	44,611	7) DAN FOUTS	5,604	7) FRAN TARKENTON	3,686	7) JOHNNY UNITAS	290	**CONSECUTIVE STARTS**	
8) DAN FOUTS	43,040	8) PEYTON MANNING	5,405	8) PEYTON MANNING	3,454	8) VINNY TESTAVERDE	275	1) JIM MARSHALL	270
9) PEYTON MANNING	41,531	9) JOE MONTANA	5,391	9) JOE MONTANA	3,409	9) JOE MONTANA	273	2) BRETT FAVRE	253
10) JOE MONTANA	40,551	10) DAVE KRIEG	5,311	10) DAN FOUTS	3,297	10) DAVE KRIEG	261	3) MICK TINGELHOFF	240
11) JOHNNY UNITAS	40,239	11) BOOMER ESIASON	5,205	11) DAVE KRIEG	3,105	11) SONNY JURGENSEN	255	4) BRUCE MATTHEWS	229
12) DAVE KRIEG	38,147	12) JOHNNY UNITAS	5,186	12) BOOMER ESIASON	2,969	12) DAN FOUTS	254	5) JIM OTTO	210
13) BOOMER ESIASON	37,920	13) JIM HART	5,076	13) KERRY COLLINS	2,918	13) DREW BLEDSOE	251		
14) JIM KELLY	35,467	14) STVE DEBERG	5,024	14) TROY AIKMAN	2,898	14) BOOMER ESIASON	247	**CONSECUTIVE TD GAMES**	
15) JIM EVERETT	34,837	15) JIM EVERETT	4,923	15) JIM KELLY	2,874	15) JOHN HADL	244	1) JOHNNY UNITAS	47
16) JIM HART	34,665	16) JIM KELLY	4,779	16) STEVE DEBERG	2,874	16) LEN DAWSON	239	2) BRETT FAVRE	36*
17) KERRY COLLINS	34,717	17) TROY AIKMAN	4,715	17) JIM EVERETT	2,841	17) JIM KELLY	237	3) DAN MARINO	30
18) STEVE DEBERG	34,241	18) JOHN HADL	4,687	18) JOHNNY UNITAS	2,830	18) GEORGE BLANDA	236	4) DAVE KREIG	28
19) JOHN HADL	33,503	19) PHIL SIMMS	4,647	19) MARK BRUNELL	2,738	19) STEVE YOUNG	232	5) CHRIS CHANDLER	27
20) PHIL SIMMS	33,462	20) JOE FERGUSON	4,519	20) STEVE MCNAIR	2,733	20) JOHN BRODIE	214	*(streak snapped Dec. 5, 2004)	

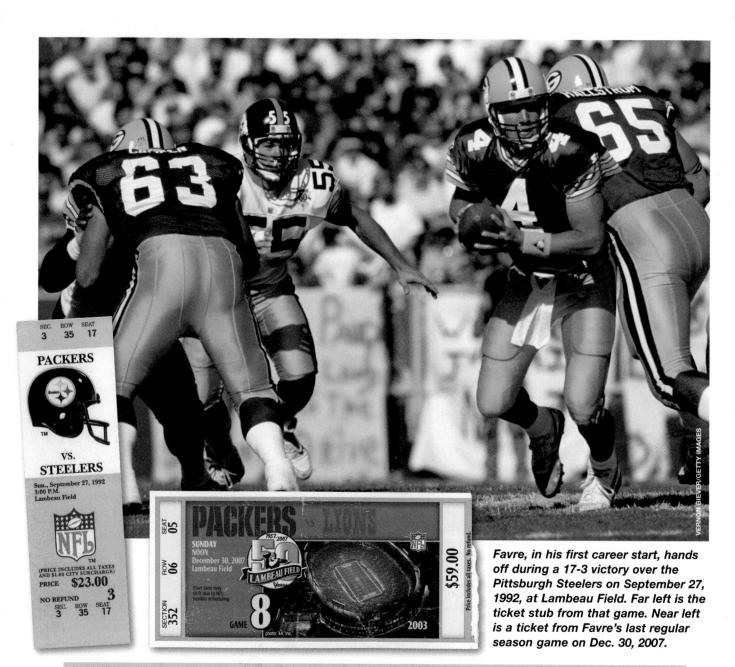

SEC. 3 ROW 35 SEAT 17

PACKERS

VS.
STEELERS

Sun., September 27, 1992
3:00 P.M.
Lambeau Field

NFL

(PRICE INCLUDES ALL TAXES AND $1.00 CITY SURCHARGE)
PRICE   **$23.00**

NO REFUND   **3**
SEC. 3 ROW 35 SEAT 17

SEAT 05 ROW 06 SECTION 352

PACKERS VS **LIONS**

SUNDAY
NOON
December 30, 2007
Lambeau Field

1957-2007
50 LAMBEAU FIELD
Years

Start time may shift due to NFL flexible scheduling

8
GAME

photo: 44, Inc.

$59.00
Price includes all taxes. No refund.

2003

Favre, in his first career start, hands off during a 17-3 victory over the Pittsburgh Steelers on September 27, 1992, at Lambeau Field. Far left is the ticket stub from that game. Near left is a ticket from Favre's last regular season game on Dec. 30, 2007.

CAREER STATS

PASSING												RUSHING					SACKED		FUMBLES	
SEASON	TEAM	G	QBRAT	COMP	ATT	PCT	YDS	Y/G	Y/A	TD	INT	RUSH	YDS	Y/G	AVG	TD	SACK	YDSL	FUM	FUML
1991	ATLANTA	2	0.0	0	5	0.0	0	0.0	0.0	0	2	0	0	0.0	0.0	0	1	11	0	0
1992	GREEN BAY	15	85.3	302	471	64.1	3227	215.1	6.9	18	13	47	198	13.2	4.2	1	34	208	0	0
1993	GREEN BAY	16	72.2	318	522	60.9	3303	206.4	6.3	19	24	58	216	13.5	3.7	1	30	199	0	0
1994	GREEN BAY	16	90.7	363	582	62.4	3882	242.6	6.7	33	14	42	202	12.6	4.8	2	31	188	6	3
1995	GREEN BAY	16	99.5	359	570	63.0	4413	275.8	7.7	38	13	39	181	11.3	4.6	3	33	217	8	4
1996	GREEN BAY	16	95.8	325	543	59.9	3899	243.7	7.2	39	13	49	136	8.5	2.8	2	40	241	10	4
1997	GREEN BAY	16	92.6	304	513	59.3	3867	241.7	7.5	35	16	58	187	11.7	3.2	1	25	176	7	4
1998	GREEN BAY	16	87.8	347	551	63.0	4212	263.3	7.6	31	23	40	133	8.3	3.3	1	38	223	8	2
1999	GREEN BAY	16	74.7	341	595	57.3	4091	255.7	6.9	22	23	28	142	8.9	5.1	0	35	223	9	4
2000	GREEN BAY	16	78.0	338	580	58.3	3812	238.3	6.6	20	16	27	108	6.8	4.0	0	33	236	9	5
2001	GREEN BAY	16	94.1	314	510	61.6	3921	245.1	7.7	32	15	38	56	3.5	1.5	1	22	151	16	6
2002	GREEN BAY	16	85.6	341	551	61.9	3658	228.6	6.6	27	16	25	73	4.6	2.9	0	26	188	10	4
2003	GREEN BAY	16	90.4	308	471	65.4	3361	210.1	7.1	32	21	18	15	0.9	0.8	0	19	137	5	2
2004	GREEN BAY	16	92.4	346	540	64.1	4088	255.5	7.6	30	17	16	36	2.3	2.3	0	12	93	4	1
2005	GREEN BAY	16	70.9	372	607	61.3	3881	242.6	6.4	20	29	18	62	3.9	3.4	0	24	170	10	7
2006	GREEN BAY	16	72.7	343	613	56.0	3885	242.8	6.3	18	18	23	29	1.8	1.3	1	21	134	7	5
2007	GREEN BAY	16	95.7	356	535	67.4	3412	284.3	7.8	28	15	29	12	.4	.4	0	14	89	8	3
CAREER		257	85.8	5377	8758	61.4	61655	240.8	7.0	442	286	555	1786	7.0	3.2	13	438	2884	117	54

Green Bay Packer fans celebrate Brett Favre's 200 consecutive starts at quarterback against the St. Louis Rams at Lambeau Field on November 29, 2004. The Packers defeated the Rams 45-17. At left is the ticket from Favre's 100th start in 1998.

NFL ALL-TIME QB RATING

			ATTEMPTS	COMPS	YARDS	TDS	INTS	RATING
1	STEVE YOUNG	NFL 15	4,149	2,667	33,124	232	107	96.8
2	PEYTON MANNING	NFL 10	5,405	3,468	41,626	306	153	94.7
3	KURT WARNER	NFL 10	2,959	1,926	24,008	152	100	93.2
4	TOM BRADY	NFL 8	3,642	2,294	26,370	197	86	92.9
5	JOE MONTANA	NFL 15	5,391	3,409	40,551	273	139	92.3
6	DAUNTE CULPEPPER	NFL 9	2,927	1,867	22,422	142	94	89.9
7	CHAD PENNINGTON	NFL 8	1,919	1,259	13,738	82	55	88.9
8	DREW BREES	NFL 7	3,015	1,921	21,189	134	82	87.9
9	JEFF GARCIA	NFL 9	3,300	2,020	22,825	149	77	87.2
10	TRENT GREEN	NFL 14	3,668	2,228	27,950	162	108	86.9
11	OTTO GRAHAM	AAFC-NFL 10	2,626	1,464	23,584	174	135	86.6
12	DAN MARINO	NFL 17	8,358	4,967	61,361	420	252	86.4
13	MATT HASSELBECK	NFL 9	3,138	1,904	22,333	142	84	86.2
14	DONOVAN MCNABB	NFL 9	3,732	2,189	25,404	171	79	85.8
15	BRETT FAVRE	NFL 17	8,758	5,377	61,655	442	288	85.7
16	RICH GANNON	NFL 17	4,206	2,533	28,743	180	104	84.7
17	JIM KELLY	NFL 11	4,779	2,874	35,467	237	175	84.4
18	MARK BRUNELL	NFL 15	4,594	2,738	31,826	182	106	84.2
19	BRIAN GRIESE	NFL 10	2,612	1,642	18,367	114	92	83.6
20	ROGER STAUBACH	NFL 11	2,958	1,685	22,700	153	09	83.4
21	BRAD JOHNSON	NFL 16	4,248	2,627	28,627	164	117	83.1

Note: Minimum 1,500 Attempts

DAVID DRAPKIN/GETTY IMAGES

Favre looks for a receiver down field against the New York Giants at Giants Stadium on September 16, 2007 in East Rutherford, N.J. The Packers defeated the Giants 35-13 as Favre established a new mark for wins by a quarterback. At right is the stadium program from the game.

GREEN BAY PACKERS RECORDS

CAREER GAMES PLAYED

1) BRETT FAVRE	255
2) BART STARR	196
3) RAY NITSCHKE	190
4) FORREST GREGG	187
5) LEROY BUTLER	181

CAREER PASSING ATTEMPTS

1) BRETT FAVRE	8,754
2) BART STARR	3,149
3) LYNN DICKEY	2,831
4) TOBIN ROTE	1,854
5) DON MAJKOWSKI	1,607

CAREER TOUCHDOWN PASSES

1) BRETT FAVRE	442
2) BART STARR	152
3) LYNN DICKEY	133
4) TOBIN ROTE	89
5) ARNIE HERBER	66

CAREER PASSING YARDS

1) BRETT FAVRE	61,655
2) BART STARR	24,718
3) LYNN DICKEY	21,369
4) TOBIN ROTE	11,535
5) DON MAJKOWSKI	10,870

CAREER COMPLETIONS

1) BRETT FAVRE	5,377
2) BART STARR	1,808
3) LYNN DICKEY	1,592
4) DON MAJKOWSKI	889
5) TOBIN ROTE	826

Note: records are for regular season only.

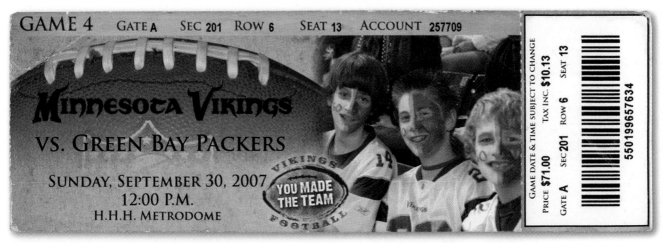

GAME 4 GATE A SEC 201 ROW 6 SEAT 13 ACCOUNT 257709

MINNESOTA VIKINGS
VS. GREEN BAY PACKERS

SUNDAY, SEPTEMBER 30, 2007
12:00 P.M.
H.H.H. METRODOME

YOU MADE THE TEAM

GAME DATE & TIME SUBJECT TO CHANGE
PRICE $71.00 TAX INC. $10.13
GATE A SEC 201 ROW 6 SEAT 13
55019965763.4

Favre established NFL marks for TD passes and passing attempts Sept. 30, 2007, at Minnesota.

Favre's longest completion, 99 yards to Robert Brooks, came at Chicago on Sept. 11, 1995.

'85 FLASHBACK

BEARS
CHICAGO BEARS
The Hardware
SEC 27 ROW 23 SEAT 5
978001-6
PACKERS
GAME 4
8:00 PM MONDAY • SEPT 11, 1995
SOLDIER FIELD

FAVRE'S STATS IN PLAYOFF GAMES

1993 SEASON

Jan. 8, 1994 (Wild Card): 28-24 win over the Lions at Detroit. Favre's line: 15 of 26, 204 yards, 3 TDs (all to Sterling Sharpe), 1 INT.

Jan. 16, 1994 (Divisional): 27-17 loss to the Cowboys at Dallas. Favre's line: 28 of 45, 331 yards, 2 TDs (1 to Robert Brooks and 1 to Sharpe), 2 INTs.

1994 SEASON

Dec. 31, 1994 (Wild Card): 16-12 win over Detroit at Lambeau Field. Favre's line: 23 of 38, 262 yards, 0 TDs, 0 INTs.

Jan. 8, 1995 (Divisional): 35-9 loss to the Cowboys at Dallas. Favre's line: 18 of 35, 211 yards, 0 TDs, 1 INT.

1995 SEASON

Dec. 31, 1995 (Wild Card): 37-20 win over Atlanta at Lambeau Field. Favre's line: 24 of 35, 199 yards, 3 TDs (1 each to Robert Brooks, Mark Chmura and Dorsey Levens), 0 INTs.

Jan. 6, 1996 (Divisional): 27-17 win over the 49ers at San Francisco. Favre's line: 21 of 28, 299 yards, 2 TDs (1 each to Keith Jackson and Chmura), 0 INTs.

Jan. 14, 1996 (NFC Championship): 38-27 loss to the Cowboys at Dallas. Favre's line: 21 of 39, 307 yards, 3 TDs (2 to Brooks and 1 to Jackson), 2 INTS.

1996 SEASON

Jan. 4, 1997 (Divisional): 35-14 win over San Francisco at Lambeau Field. Favre's line: 11 of 15, 79 yards, 1 TD (to Andre Rison), 0 INT.

Jan. 12, 1997 (NFC Championship): 30-13 win over Carolina at Lambeau Field. Favre's line: 19 of 29, 292 yards, 2 TDs (1 to Dorsey Levens and 1 to Antonio Freeman), 1 INT.

Jan. 26, 1997 (Super Bowl XXXI): 35-21 win over New England at New Orleans Superdome. Favre's line: 14 of 27, 246 yards, 2 TDs (1 to Rison and 1 to Freeman), 0 INTs.

1997 SEASON

Jan. 4, 1998 (Divisional): 21-7 win over Tampa Bay at Lambeau Field. Favre's line 15

of 28, 190 yards, 1 TD (to Chmura), 2 INTs.

Jan. 11, 1998 (NFC Championship): 23-10 win over the 49ers at San Francisco. Favre's line: 16 of 27, 222 yards, 1 TD (Freeman), 0 INT.

Jan. 25, 1998 (Super Bowl XXXII): 31-24 loss to Denver at San Diego. Favre's line: 25 of 42, 256 yards, 3 TDs (2 to Freeman and 1 to Mark Chmura), 1 INT.

1998 SEASON

Jan. 3, 1999 (Wild Card): 30-27 loss at San Francisco. Favre's line: 20 of 35, 292 yards, 2 TDs (both to Freeman), 2 INTs.

2001 SEASON

Jan. 13, 2002 (Wild Card): 25-15 win over San Francisco at Lambeau Field. Favre's line: 22 of 29, 269 yards, 2 TDs (to Bubba Franks and Freeman), 1 INT.

Jan. 20, 2002 (Divisional): 45-17 loss at St. Louis. Favre's line: 26 of 44, 281 yards, 2 TDs (both to Freeman), 5 INTs.

2002 SEASON

Jan. 4, 2003 (Wild Card): 27-7 loss to Atlanta at Lambeau Field. Favre's line: 20 of 42, 247 yards, 1 TD (to Donald Driver), 2 INTs.

2003 SEASON

Jan. 4, 2004 (Wild Card): 33-27 OT win over Seattle at Lambeau Field. Favre's line: 26 of 38, 319 yards, 1 TD (to Franks), 0 INT.

Jan. 11, 2004 (Divisional): 20-17 loss at Philadelphia. Favre's line: 15 of 28, 180 yards, 2 TDs (2 to Robert Ferguson).

2004 SEASON

Jan. 9, 2005 (Wild Card): 31-17 loss to Minnesota at Lambeau Field. Favre's line: 22 of 33, 216 yards, 1 TD (Franks), 4 INTs.

2007 SEASON

Jan. 12, 2008 (Divisional Round): 42-20 win over Seattle at Lambeau Field. Favre's line: 18 of 23, 173 yards, 3 TDs, 0 Ints.

Jan. 20, 2008 (NFC Championship): 23-20 loss to New York Giants at Lambeau Field. Favre's line: 19 of 35, 235 yards, 2 TDs, 2 Ints.

Consistently Great

College & 1991

Team	Games	Att	Cmp	Yds	Cmp%	Y/Att	TD	Int
Southern Miss	42	1,169	613	7,695	52.4	6.6	52	34
Atlanta Falcons	2	5	0	0	0	0	0	2

Favre Highlights

Led Southern Mississippi to 29 victories in four seasons, including two bowl wins. Won Most Valuable Player award in both the East-West Shrine game and the All-American Bowl. Set school records for passing yards (8,193), pass attempts (1,234), completions (656), passing percentage (53.0) and touchdowns (55), with only 35 interceptions.

Shocked his coaches and teammates by returning to the starting lineup a month after a car accident and abdominal surgery to escort the Golden Eagles to an upset over Alabama. Also was MVP of All-American Bowl at conclusion of senior year. Saw action briefly in two games with the Atlanta Falcons as a rookie after being drafted in the second round, but did not complete a pass.

ALLEN STEELE/GETTY IMAGES

ALLEN STEELE/GETTY IMAGES

Did You Know?

● Favre finished his college career ranked in the NCAA's top 30 all-time in passing yards with 7,695.

By The Numbers...

0 The number of completions to his teammates his rookie year with the Falcons.

2 The number of completions to opponents his rookie year with the Falcons.

Head coach Jerry Glanville referred to Favre as a "car wreck," and that basically summed up his mistake-prone year in Atlanta. The Falcons traded Favre to the Packers for a first-round draft choice at the end of the 1991 season.

CONSISTENTLY GREAT **31**

1992

Team	Games	Att	Cmp	Yds	Cmp%	Y/Att	TD	Int	Rate
Green Bay	15	471	302	3,227	64.1	6.9	18	13	85.3

Favre Highlights

Entered the game in the third week when Don Majkowski was injured and led the team to a come-from-behind 24-23 win over Cincinnati with a 35-yard scoring pass to wideout Kitrick Taylor with only 13 seconds remaining in the game.

Went 8-5 as a starter and established two new Green Bay passing records – single-season marks for passing percentage (64.12 percent, since broken) and most consecutive 200-yard passing games (11).

VERNON BIEVER /NFL PHOTOS/GETTY IMAGES

VERNON BIEVER /NFL PHOTOS/GETTY IMAGES

Team Summary

Record: 9-7
Playoffs: Missed Playoffs
Highlights: Vince Workman led the team in rushing with 631 yards. Sterling Sharpe had 108 catches for 1,461 yards and 13 touchdowns; the rest of the team combined for seven TD catches. The Packers won six games in a row down the stretch and challenged for a playoff spot before losing 27-7 at Minnesota in the season finale.

GAME	DATE	OPPONENT	W/L	GB	Op.	LOCATION
1.	09-06-92	Minnesota Vikings	L	20	23	Home
2.	09-13-92	Tampa Bay Buccaneers	L	3	31	Away
3.	09-20-92	Cincinnati Bengals	W	24	23	Home
4.	09-27-92	Pittsburgh Steelers	W	17	3	Home
5.	10-04-92	Atlanta Falcons	L	10	24	Away
6.	10-18-92	Cleveland Browns	L	6	17	Away
7.	10-25-92	Chicago Bears	L	10	30	Home
8.	11-01-92	Detroit Lions	W	27	13	Away
9.	11-08-92	New York Giants	L	7	27	Away
10.	11-15-92	Philadelphia Eagles	W	27	24	Home (Milw)
11.	11-22-92	Chicago Bears	W	17	3	Away
12.	11-29-92	Tampa Bay Buccaneers	W	19	14	Home (Milw)
13.	12-06-92	Detroit Lions	W	38	10	Home (Milw)
14.	12-13-92	Houston Oilers	W	16	14	Away
15.	12-20-92	Los Angeles Rams	W	28	13	Home
16.	12-27-92	Minnesota Vikings	L	7	27	Away

One of Mike Holmgren's claims to fame was that he coached both Joe Montana and Steve Young in San Francisco. The experience did little to prepare Holmgren for what was in store for him in Green Bay with the freewheeling Favre.

By The Numbers...

11 On Jan. 11, San Francisco offensive coordinator Mike Holmgren was named the 11th head coach in Packers history.

111 Favre had a string of 111 passes without an interception in his first full season as a starter.

1 Atlanta acquired a first-round draft pick from Green Bay for Favre.

1992

LC LARRY LAMBRECHT/NFL/GETTY IMAGES

ANDY HAYT/GETTY IMAGES

TOM G. LYNN/TIME LIFE PICTURES/GETTY IMAGES

ROSTER

No	Name	Pos	Ht	Wt	DOB	College	G
4	Favre, Brett	QB	6-2	220	10/10/69	Southern Mississippi	15
7	Majkowski, Don	QB	6-2	203	02/25/64	Virginia	14
9	Wagner, Bryan	P	6-2	200	03/28/62	Cal State-Northridge	7
13	Jacke, Chris	K	6-0	197	03/12/66	Texas-El Paso	16
16	McJulien, Paul	P	5-10	210	02/24/65	Jackson State	9
21	Carter, Carl	CB	5-11	190	03/07/64	Texas Tech	7
22	Billups, Lewis	CB	5-11	182	10/10/63	North Alabama	5
23	McCloughan, Dave	CB	6-1	185	11/20/66	Colorado	5
24	Hauck, Tim	S	5-10	181	12/20/66	Montana	16
25	Clark, Vinnie	CB	6-0	194	01/22/69	Ohio State	16
26	Cecil, Chuck	S	6-0	190	11/08/64	Arizona	16
27	Buckley, Terrell	CB	5-9	174	06/07/71	Florida State	14
29	Wilson, Marcus	RB	6-1	210	04/16/68	Virginia	6
31	McGee, Buford	RB	6-0	210	08/16/60	Mississippi	4
34	Bennett, Edgar	RB	6-0	223	02/15/69	Florida State	16
36	Butler, LeRoy	S	6-0	200	07/19/68	Florida State	15
38	White, Adrian	S	6-0	205	04/06/64	Florida	15
39	Thompson, Darrell	RB	6-0	222	11/23/67	Minnesota	7
40	Jackson, Johnnie	S	6-1	204	01/11/67	Houston	1
42	Sydney, Harry	FB	6-0	217	06/29/59	Kansas	16
45	McNabb, Dexter	FB	6-1	245	07/09/69	Florida	16
46	Workman, Vince	RB	5-10	205	05/09/68	Ohio State	10
47	Mitchell, Roland	CB	5-11	195	03/15/64	Texas Tech	15
50	Holland, Johnny	LB	6-2	235	03/11/65	Texas A&M	14
51	Brady, Jeff	LB	6-1	235	11/09/68	Kentucky	8
52	Winters, Frank	C	6-3	290	01/23/64	West Illinois	16
53	Koonce, George	LB	6-1	238	10/15/68	East Carolina	16
55	Collins, Brett	LB	6-1	226	10/08/68	Washington	11
56	Dent, Burnell	LB	6-1	238	03/16/63	Tulane	15
57	Moran, Rich	G	6-2	280	03/19/62	San Diego State	8
58	D'Onofrio, Mark	LB	6-2	235	03/17/69	Penn State	2
61	Neville, Tom	G	6-5	288	09/04/61	Fresno State	8
62	Brock, Matt	DE	6-4	290	01/14/66	Oregon	16
63	Campen, James	C	6-3	280	06/11/64	Tulane	13
65	Hallstrom, Ron	G	6-6	310	06/11/59	Iowa	16
67	Barrie, Sebastian	DE	6-2	270	05/26/70	Liberty University	3
68	Sims, Joe	OL	6-3	294	03/01/69	Nebraska	15
71	Gray, Cecil	T	6-4	292	02/16/68	North Carolina	2
72	Salem, Harvey	T	6-6	289	01/15/61	California	4
73	Robbins, Tootie	T	6-5	315	06/02/58	East Carolina	15
74	Archambeau, Lester	DE	6-4	270	06/27/67	Stanford	16
75	Ruettgers, Ken	T	6-5	286	08/20/62	USC	16
76	Viaene, David	OL	6-5	300	07/14/65	Minnesota-Duluth	1
77	Millard, Keith	DT	6-5	268	03/18/62	Washington State	2
80	Harris, Jackie	TE	6-3	243	01/04/68	North Louisiana	16
81	Harris, Corey	WR	5-11	195	10/25/69	Vanderbilt	10
82	Beach, Sanjay	WR	6-1	194	02/21/66	Colorado State	16
84	Sharpe, Sterling	WR	5-11	205	04/06/65	South Carolina	16
85	Lewis, Ron	WR	5-11	180	03/25/68	Florida State	6
85	Taylor, Kitrick	WR	5-11	189	07/22/64	Washington State	10
86	West, Ed	TE	6-1	244	08/02/61	Auburn	16
87	Brooks, Robert	WR	6-0	171	06/23/70	South Carolina	16
88	Ingram, Darryl	TE	6-3	250	05/02/66	California	16
90	Bennett, Tony	LB	6-2	243	07/01/67	Mississippi	16
91	Noble, Brian	LB	6-3	250	09/06/62	Arizona State	13
92	Jurkovic, John	NT	6-2	300	08/18/67	Eastern Illinois	16
93	Brown, Robert	DE	6-2	280	05/21/60	Virginia Tech	16
95	Paup, Bryce	LB	6-4	247	02/29/68	Northern Iowa	16
97	Noonan, Danny	NT	6-4	275	07/14/65	Nebraska	6
98	Oglesby, Alfred	NT	6-3	285	01/27/67	Houston	7
98	Tuaolo, Esera	NT	6-2	284	07/11/68	Oregon State	4
99	Davey, Don	DE	6-4	280	04/08/68	Wisconsin	9

DRAFT

Rnd	Name	Pos	Ht	Wt	College
1a	Terrell Buckley (5)	DB	5-9	174	Florida State
1b	(Choice (17) from Eagles in 1991 position exchange. Choice traded to Falcons for Brett Favre)				
2a	Mark D'Onofrio (34)	LB	6-2	235	Penn State
2b	(Choice (45) from 49ers for Tim Harris. Choice returned to 49ers for right to hire Mike Holmgren)				
3	Robert Brooks (62)	WR	6-0	171	South Carolina
4a	(Choice (89) and 8th round pick (203) to 49ers for 49ers' 4th round pick (103), 5th round pick (130) and 6th round pick (157))				
4b	Edgar Bennett (103)	RB	6-0	223	Florida State
	(Choice from 49ers in exchange mentioned above)				
5a	Dexter McNabb (119)	FB	6-1	245	Florida
5b	Orlando McKay (130)	WR	5-10	175	Washington
	(Choice from 49ers in exchange mentioned above)				

Rnd	Name	Pos	Ht	Wt	College
6a	(Choice (146) to Phoenix for Tootie Robbins)				
6b	Mark Chmura (157)	TE	6-5	240	Boston College
	(Choice from 49ers in exchange mentioned above)				
7a	(Choice (173) to the Raiders for Raiders' 7th round choice (190) and 9th round choice (240))				
7b	Chris Holder (190)	WR	6-0	182	Tuskegee
	(Choice from Raiders in exchange mentioned above)				
8	(Choice (203) to 49ers in exchange mentioned above)				
9a	Ty Detmer (230)	QB	5-9	183	BYU
9b	Shazzon Bradley (240)	NT	6-1	272	Tennessee
	(Choice from Raiders in exchange mentioned above)				
10	Andrew Oberg (257)	T	6-6	300	North Carolina
11	Gabe Mokwuah (287)	LB	6-1	254	Am. International
12	Brett Collins (314)	LB	6-1	226	Washington

FRONT ROW: (L-R) 4 Brett Favre, 7 Don Majkowski, 11 Ty Detmer, 13 Chris Jacke, 16 Paul McJulien, 22 Lewis Billups, 23 Dave McCloughan, 24 Tim Hauck, 25 Vinnie Clark, 26 Chuck Cecil, 27 Terrell Buckley.
SECOND ROW: (L-R) 29 Marcus Wilson, 31 Buford McGee, 34 Edgar Bennett, 36 LeRoy Butler, 38 Adrian White, 39 Darrell Thompson, 42 Harry Sydney, 45 Dexter McNabb, 46 Vince Workman, 47 Roland Mitchell, 50 Johnny Holland, 51 Jeff Brady.
THIRD ROW: (L-R) 52 Frank Winters, 53 George Koonce, 55 Brett Collins, 56 Burnell Dent, 57 Rich Moran, 62 Matt Brock, 63 James Campen, 65 Ron Hallstrom, 68 Joe Sims, 69 Joe Garten, 72 Harvey Salem.
FOURTH ROW: (L-R) 73 Tootie Robbins, 74 Lester Archambeau, 75 Ken Ruettgers, 79 Tony Mandarich, 80 Jackie Harris, 82 Sanjay Beach, 83 Orlando McKay, 84 Sterling Sharpe, 85 Kitrick Taylor, 86 Ed West, 87 Robert Brooks.
FIFTH ROW: (L-R) 88 Daryl Ingram, 89 Mark Chmura, 90 Tony Bennett, 91 Brian Noble, 92 John Jurkovic, 93 Robert Brown, 94 Mark D'Onofrio, 95 Bryce Paup, 96 Shawn Patterson, 97 Danny Noonan, 98 Esera Tuaolo.
SIXTH ROW: (L-R) Defensive Assistant/Quality Control Jim Lind, Tight Ends/Assistant Offensive Line Coach Tom Lovat, Quarterbacks Coach Steve Mariucci, Special Teams Coach Nolan Cromwell, Offensive Coordinator Sherman Lewis, Head Coach Mike Holmgren, Defensive Coordinator Ray Rhodes, Defensive Line Coach Greg Blache, Linebackers Coach Bob Valesente, Offensive Assistant/Quality Control Jon Gruden, Strength and Conditioning Kent Johnston, Defensive Backs Coach Dick Jauron, Running Backs Coach Gil Haskell.
BACK ROW: (L-R) Equipment Assistant Jack Noel, Assistant Equipment Manager Bryan Nehring, Equipment Manager Bob Noel, Administrative Assistant John Johnson, Head Trainer Domenic Gentile, Assistant Trainer Kurt Fielding, Assistant Trainer Jay Davide, Training Room Intern Sam Ramsden, Staff Orthopedist Dr. Patrick J. McKenzie, Team Physician Dr. Clarence G. Novotny, Assistant Video Director Bob Eckberg, Video Director Al Treml.

1993

Team	Games	Att	Cmp	Yds	Cmp%	Y/Att	TD	Int	Rate
Green Bay	16	522	318	3,303	60.9	6.3	19	24	72.2

Favre Highlights

One of Favre's greatest plays ever came in his first playoff game, when he threw a spectacular 40-yard touchdown pass to Sterling Sharpe to win at Detroit 28-24. He then had 331 yards passing and two touchdowns as the Packers lost the following week 27-17 at Dallas.

Played in the Pro Bowl for the second time in two seasons as a starter. Established himself as a come-from-behind quarterback with two late TDs in three weeks, at New Orleans and vs. Tampa Bay.

JONATHAN DANIEL/GETTY IMAGES

JONATHAN DANIEL/GETTY IMAGES

Team Summary

Record: 9-7, Wild Card

Playoffs: Won on late TD pass to Sterling Sharpe in first round at Detroit for first playoff win in over a decade, lost in second round to renewed rival Dallas. The Packers and Lions faced each other at the Silverdome in consecutive weeks, with the Lions winning the season finale 30-20 to gain homefield advantage, but the Packers exacting payback the following week in the first round of the postseason.

Highlights: Darrell Thompson was leading rusher, with 654 yards. Sterling Sharpe had 112 catches for 1,274 yards and 11 TDs.

GAME	DATE	OPPONENT	W/L	GB	Op.	LOCATION
1.	09-05-93	Los Angeles Rams	Win	36	6	Home (Milw)
2.	09-12-93	Philadelphia Eagles	Loss	17	20	Home
3.	09-26-93	Minnesota Vikings	Loss	13	15	Away
4.	10-03-93	Dallas Cowboys	Loss	14	36	Away
5.	10-10-93	Denver Broncos	Win	30	27	Home
6.	10-24-93	Tampa Bay Buccaneers	Win	37	14	Away
7.	10-31-93	Chicago Bears	Win	17	3	Home
8.	11-08-93	Kansas City Chiefs	Loss	16	23	Away
9.	11-14-93	New Orleans Saints	Win	19	17	Away
10.	11-21-93	Detroit Lions	Win	26	17	Home (Milw)
11.	11-28-93	Tampa Bay Buccaneers	Win	13	10	Home
12.	12-05-93	Chicago Bears	Loss	17	30	Away
13.	12-12-93	San Diego Chargers	Win	20	13	Away
14.	12-19-93	Minnesota Vikings	Loss	17	21	Home (Milw)
15.	12-26-93	Los Angeles Raiders	Win	28	0	Home
16.	01-02-94	Detroit Lions	Loss	20	30	Away
17.	01-08-94	Detroit Lions	Win	28	24	Away
18.	01-16-94	Dallas Cowboys	Loss	17	27	Away

Favre proved both frustrating and amazing during his second season in Green Bay, throwing 24 interceptions yet leading the Packers to victory in the play-offs for the first time in 10 years.

By The Numbers...

4 Favre's first four-TD passing game came at Tampa Bay on Oct. 24, and all four TDs were to Sterling Sharpe.

36 Set the team's single-game completion record at Chicago Dec. 5, beating Lynn Dickey's 35.

402 Became the third Green Bay quarterback to throw for 400 yards, also at Chicago.

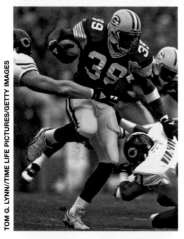

TOM G. LYNN/TIME LIFE PICTURES/GETTY IMAGES

TODD ROSENBERG/GETTY IMAGES

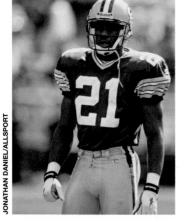

JONATHAN DANIEL/ALLSPORT

ROSTER

No	Name	Pos	Ht	Wt	DOB	College	G
4	Favre, Brett	QB	6-2	222	10/10/69	Southern Mississippi	16
9	Wagner, Bryan	P	6-2	200	03/28/62	Cal State-Northridge	3
11	Detmer, Ty	QB	6-0	186	10/30/67	BYU	3
13	Jacke, Chris	K	6-0	200	03/12/66	Texas-El Paso	16
20	Williams, Kevin	RB	6-1	215	02/17/70	UCLA	3
23	Walker, Sammy	CB	5-11	200	01/20/69	Texas Tech	8
24	Hauck, Tim	S	5-10	187	12/20/66	Montana	13
25	Oliver, Muhammad	CB	5-11	180	03/12/69	Oregon	2
27	Buckley, Terrell	CB	5-9	176	06/07/71	Florida State	16
29	Wilson, Marcus	RB	6-1	210	04/16/68	Virginia	16
30	Harris, Corey	CB	5-11	195	10/25/69	Vanderbilt	11
31	Teague, George	S	6-1	187	02/18/71	Alabama	16
32	Stephens, John	RB	6-1	215	02/23/66	Northwestern (LA) State	5
33	Evans, Doug	CB	6-1	188	05/13/70	Louisiana Tech	16
34	Bennett, Edgar	RB	6-0	224	02/15/69	Florida State	16
36	Butler, LeRoy	S	6-0	197	07/19/68	Florida State	16
38	Pickens, Bruce	CB	5-11	190	05/09/68	Nebraska	2
39	Thompson, Darrell	RB	6-0	217	11/23/67	Minnesota	16
45	McNabb, Dexter	FB	6-1	245	07/09/69	Florida	16
45	Prior, Mike	S	6-0	215	11/14/63	Illinois State	16
47	Mitchell, Roland	CB	5-11	195	03/15/64	Texas Tech	16
50	Holland, Johnny	LB	6-2	235	03/11/65	Texas A&M	16
51	Morrissey, Jim	LB	6-3	225	12/24/62	Michigan State	6
52	Winters, Frank	C	6-3	290	01/23/64	West Illinois	16
53	Koonce, George	LB	6-1	240	10/15/68	East Carolina	15
54	Coleman, Keo	LB	6-1	245	05/01/70	Mississippi State	12
55	Collins, Brett	LB	6-1	234	10/08/68	Washington	4
55	Mott, Joe	LB	6-4	255	10/06/65	Iowa	2
56	Willis, James	LB	6-1	238	09/02/72	Auburn	13
57	Moran, Rich	G	6-2	280	03/19/62	San Diego State	3
59	Simmons, Wayne	LB	6-2	245	12/15/69	Clemson	14
60	Zeno, Lance	C	6-4	279	04/15/67	UCLA	5
62	Brock, Matt	DE	6-4	290	01/14/66	Oregon	16
63	Campen, James	C	6-3	280	06/11/64	Tulane	4
64	Jurkovic, John	NT	6-2	290	08/18/67	Eastern Illinois	16
67	Hutchins, Paul	T	6-4	335	02/11/70	Western Michigan	1
68	Sims, Joe	OL	6-3	310	03/01/69	Nebraska	13
70	Grant, David	NT	6-4	275	09/17/65	West Virginia	7
72	Dotson, Earl	T	6-3	310	12/17/70	Texas A&I	13
73	Robbins, Tootie	T	6-5	315	06/02/58	East Carolina	12
74	Widell, Doug	G	6-4	287	09/23/66	Boston College	16
75	Ruettgers, Ken	T	6-5	290	08/20/62	USC	16
76	Galbreath, Harry	G	6-1	285	01/01/65	Tennessee	16
77	Maas, Bill	NT	6-5	282	03/02/62	Pittsburgh	14
79	Ilkin, Tunch	T	6-3	272	09/23/57	Indiana State	1
80	Harris, Jackie	TE	6-3	243	01/04/68	North Louisiana	12
81	Collins, Shawn	WR	6-2	205	02/20/67	Northern Arizona	4
81	Morgan, Anthony	WR	6-1	195	11/15/67	Tennessee	2
83	Clayton, Mark	WR	5-9	185	04/08/61	Louisville	16
84	Sharpe, Sterling	WR	5-11	210	04/06/65	South Carolina	16
85	Lewis, Ron	WR	5-11	192	03/25/68	Florida State	9
86	West, Ed	TE	6-1	245	08/02/61	Auburn	16
87	Brooks, Robert	WR	6-0	175	06/23/70	South Carolina	14
88	Ingram, Darryl	TE	6-3	245	05/02/66	California	2
89	Chmura, Mark	TE	6-5	245	02/22/69	Boston College	14
90	Bennett, Tony	LB	6-2	243	07/01/67	Mississippi	10
91	Noble, Brian	LB	6-3	245	09/06/62	Arizona State	2
92	White, Reggie	DE	6-5	295	12/19/61	Tennessee	16
93	Brown, Gilbert	NT	6-2	330	02/22/71	Kansas	2
95	Paup, Bryce	LB	6-4	247	02/29/68	Northern Iowa	15
96	Patterson, Shawn	DE	6-5	270	06/13/64	Arizona State	5
97	Traylor, Keith	DE	6-2	290	09/03/69	Central Oklahoma	5
99	Davey, Don	DE	6-4	270	04/08/68	Wisconsin	9

DRAFT

Rnd	Name	Pos	Ht	Wt	College
1a	Wayne Simmons (15)	LB	6-2	236	Louisiana Tech
1b	George Teague (29)	DB	6-1	185	Alabama

(Packers traded two 2nd-rd choices (46 & 54), a 4th-rd pick (94) and an 8th-rd pick (213) to the Cowboys for the Cowboys' 1st-round choice (29) and 4th-rd pick (112))

2a	(Choice (46) traded to the Cowboys in deal mentioned above)
2b	(Choice (54) from 49ers for Tim Harris; to Cowboys in deal mentioned above)
3a	(Choice (72) to Raiders for Raiders' 3rd-rd pick (81) and 6th-rd pick (152))

| 3b | Earl Dotson (81) | T | 6-3 | 318 | Texas A&I |

(Choice from Raiders in deal mentioned above)

4a	(Choice (94) from Falcons for Vinnie Clark; to Cowboys in deal above)
4b	(Choice (99) to Patriots for John Stephens)
4c	(Choice (112) from Cowboys in deal mentioned above; to Bears for Bears'-5th-round pick (118) and 6th-round pick (156))

Rnd	Name	Pos	Ht	Wt	College
5a	Mark Brunell (118)	QB	6-1	206	Washington

(Choice from Bears in deal mentioned above)

| 5b | James Willis (119) | LB | 6-1 | 230 | Auburn |

(Choice from Buccaneers for signing Vince Workman)

| 5c | (Choice (129) to Jets for Ken O'Brien) |
| 6a | Doug Evans (141) | CB | 6-1 | 186 | Louisiana Tech |

(Choice from Seahawks for Doug McCloughan)

| 6b | Paul Hutchins (152) | T | 6-4 | 347 | Western Michigan |

(Choice from Raiders in deal mentioned above)

| 6c | Tim Watson (156) | SS | 6-2 | 215 | Howard |

(Choice (156) traded to Colts for Dave McCloughan.
Colts traded choice to Bears who traded it back to Packers in the deal mentioned above)

| 7 | Robert Kuberski (183) | DT | 6-4 | 281 | Naval Academy |
| 8 | (Choice (213) to Cowboys in deal mentioned above) |

The best thing that could be said about the Packers' running game in 1993 is that Favre threw the ball a lot. Darrell Thompson led the team with only 654 yards rushing.

1994

Team	Games	Att	Cmp	Yds	Cmp%	Y/Att	TD	Int	Rate
Green Bay	16	582	363	3,882	62.4	6.7	33	14	90.7

Favre Highlights

The final game ever in Milwaukee was memorable for Favre's diving TD with 14 seconds remaining that capped a 21-17 victory over Atlanta. The following week, he completed three TD passes to Sterling Sharpe in a playoff-clinching win at Tampa Bay, Sharpe's last game as a pro. Favre was named second team All-Pro by *Football Digest*.

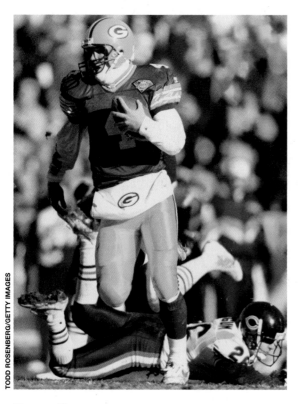

TODD ROSENBERG/GETTY IMAGES

JONATHAN DANIEL/GETTY IMAGES

Team Summary

Record: 9-7, Wild Card

Playoffs: Beat Lions in home playoff game memorable for Barry Sanders' minus-3 yards rushing, then lost at Dallas again.

Highlights: Edgar Bennett led the team with 623 yards rushing, while Sterling Sharpe had 94 catches for 1,119 yards and 18 touchdowns in his final season before having his career cut short by a spinal condition. Among the regular season high points were a pair of lopsided wins against the Bears — a memorable 33-6 road blowout on a windy, rainy Halloween night and a 40-3 thrashing of their rivals Dec. 11 at Lambeau Field.

GAME	DATE	OPPONENT	W/L	GB	Op.	LOCATION
1.	09-04-94	Minnesota Vikings	Win	16	10	Home
2.	09-11-94	Miami Dolphins	Loss	14	24	Home (Milw)
3.	09-18-94	Philadelphia Eagles	Loss	7	13	Away
4.	09-25-94	Tampa Bay Buccaneers	Win	30	3	Home
5.	10-02-94	New England Patriots	Loss	16	17	Away
6.	10-09-94	Los Angeles Rams	Win	24	17	Home
7.	10-20-94	Minnesota Vikings	Loss	10	13	Away
8.	10-31-94	Chicago Bears	Win	33	6	Away
9.	11-06-94	Detroit Lions	Win	38	30	Home (Milw)
10.	11-13-94	New York Jets	Win	17	10	Home
11.	11-20-94	Buffalo Bills	Loss	20	29	Away
12.	11-24-94	Dallas Cowboys	Loss	31	42	Away
13.	12-04-94	Detroit Lions	Loss	31	34	Away
14.	12-11-94	Chicago Bears	Win	40	3	Home
15.	12-18-94	Atlanta Falcons	Win	21	17	Home (Milw)
16.	12-24-94	Tampa Bay Buccaneers	Win	34	19	Away
17.	12-31-94	Detroit Lions	Win	16	12	Home
18.	01-08-95	Dallas Cowboys	Loss	9	35	Away

Did You Know?

● When Favre threw for four touchdowns without an interception in a loss at Dallas on Thanksgiving Day, it was against the top-ranked defense in the league.

Favre threw 33 touchdown passes in 1994, beginning a stretch of five straight years in which he tossed more than 30 scoring strikes. During that period he threw 176 touchdowns, or 24 more than Bart Starr threw during his career.

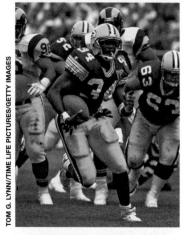

ROSTER

No	Name	Pos	Ht	Wt	DOB	College	G
4	Favre, Brett	QB	6-2	222	10/10/69	Southern Mississippi	16
8	Brunell, Mark	QB	6-1	208	09/17/70	Washington	2
13	Jacke, Chris	K	6-0	200	03/12/66	Texas-El Paso	16
17	Hentrich, Craig	P	6-3	200	05/18/71	Notre Dame	16
21	Duckett, Forey	CB	6-3	195	02/05/70	Nevada-Reno	3
22	McGill, Lenny	CB	6-1	194	05/31/71	Arizona State	6
24	Hauck, Tim	S	5-10	187	12/20/66	Montana	13
25	Levens, Dorsey	RB	6-1	235	05/21/70	Georgia Tech	14
26	Thompson, Darrell	RB	6-0	217	11/23/67	Minnesota	8
27	Buckley, Terrell	CB	5-9	176	06/07/71	Florida State	16
29	Wilson, Marcus	RB	6-1	210	04/16/68	Virginia	12
30	Harris, Corey	CB	5-11	195	10/25/69	Vanderbilt	16
31	Teague, George	S	6-1	187	02/18/71	Alabama	16
32	Cobb, Reggie	RB	6-0	215	07/07/68	Tennessee	16
33	Evans, Doug	CB	6-1	188	05/13/70	Louisiana Tech	16
34	Bennett, Edgar	RB	6-0	224	02/15/69	Florida State	16
35	Wilson, Ray	S	6-2	202	08/26/71	New Mexico	3
36	Butler, LeRoy	S	6-0	197	07/19/68	Florida State	13
37	Johnson, KeShon	CB	5-10	179	07/17/70	Arizona	7
39	Prior, Mike	S	6-0	215	11/14/63	Illinois State	16
42	Johnson, LeShon	RB	5-11	200	01/15/71	Northern Illinois	12
47	Mitchell, Roland	CB	5-11	195	03/15/64	Texas Tech	1
51	Williams, Mark	LB	6-3	240	05/17/71	Ohio State	16
52	Winters, Frank	C	6-3	290	01/23/64	West Illinois	16
53	Koonce, George	LB	6-1	240	10/15/68	East Carolina	16
55	Strickland, Fred	LB	6-2	250	08/15/66	Purdue	16
56	Willis, James	LB	6-1	238	09/02/72	Auburn	12
58	Hamilton, Ruffin	LB	6-1	230	03/02/71	Tulane	5
59	Simmons, Wayne	LB	6-2	245	12/15/69	Clemson	12
62	McIntyre, Guy	G	6-3	265	02/17/61	Georgia	10
63	Dukes, Jamie	C	6-1	295	06/14/64	Florida State	6
64	Jurkovic, John	NT	6-2	290	08/18/67	Eastern Illinois	16
67	Hutchins, Paul	T	6-4	335	02/11/70	Western Michigan	16
68	Sims, Joe	OL	6-3	310	03/01/69	Nebraska	15
70	Hope, Charles	G	6-3	303	03/12/70	Central State	6
71	Brown, Gary	T	6-4	288	06/25/71	Georgia Tech	1
72	Dotson, Earl	T	6-3	310	12/17/70	Texas A&I	4
75	Ruettgers, Ken	T	6-5	290	08/20/62	USC	16
76	Galbreath, Harry	G	6-1	285	01/01/65	Tennessee	16
80	Jordan, Charles	WR	5-10	175	10/09/69	Long Beach City College	10
81	Morgan, Anthony	WR	6-1	195	11/15/67	Tennessee	16
82	Johnson, Reggie	TE	6-2	256	01/27/68	Florida State	9
83	Wilner, Jeff	TE	6-4	250	12/31/71	Wesleyan	11
84	Sharpe, Sterling	WR	5-11	210	04/06/65	South Carolina	16
85	Lewis, Ron	WR	5-11	192	03/25/68	Florida State	6
86	West, Ed	TE	6-1	245	08/02/61	Auburn	14
87	Brooks, Robert	WR	6-0	175	06/23/70	South Carolina	16
88	Mickens, Terry	WR	6-0	200	02/21/71	Florida A&M	12
89	Chmura, Mark	TE	6-5	245	02/22/69	Boston College	14
90	McMichael, Steve	DT	6-2	270	10/17/57	Texas	16
92	White, Reggie	DE	6-5	295	12/19/61	Tennessee	16
93	Brown, Gilbert	NT	6-2	330	02/22/71	Kansas	13
94	Brock, Matt	DE	6-4	290	01/14/66	Oregon	5
95	Paup, Bryce	LB	6-4	247	02/29/68	Northern Iowa	16
96	Jones, Sean	DE	6-7	275	12/19/62	Northeastern	16
98	Wilkins, Gabe	DE	6-4	300	09/01/71	Gardner-Webb	15
99	Davey, Don	DE	6-4	270	04/08/68	Wisconsin	16

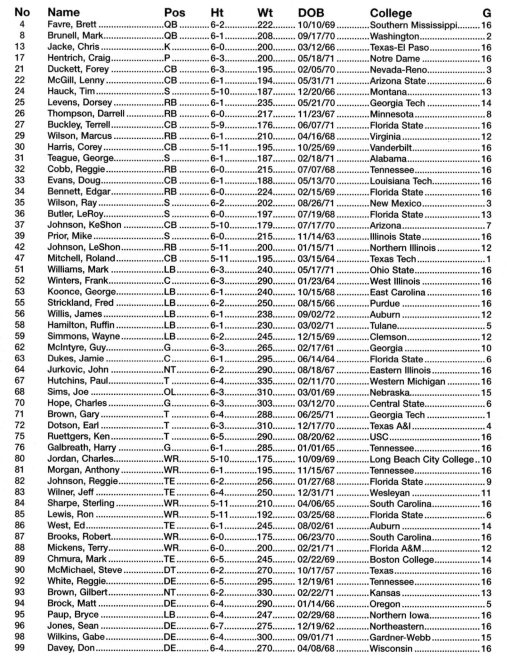

DRAFT

Rnd	Name	Pos	Ht	Wt	College
1a	Aaron Taylor (16)	G	6-4	300	Notre Dame

(Packers traded 1st-round (20) and 3rd-round (89) picks to Dolphins for Dolphins' 1st-round pick (16))

| 1b | (Choice (20) to Dolphins in deal mentioned above) | | | | |

| 2 | (Choice (53) to 49ers for 49ers' 3rd-round (84), 5th-round (149), and two 6th-round picks (175) and (190)) | | | | |

| 3a | LeShon Johnson (84) | RB | 5-11 | 200 | Northern Illinois |

(Choice from 49ers in deal mentioned above)

| 3b | (Choice (89) to Dolphins in deal mentioned above) | | | | |

| 4a | (Choice (120) to Raiders for Raiders' 4th-round (126) and 6th-round (169) picks) | | | | |

| 4b | Gabe Wilkins (126) | DE | 6-4 | 300 | Gardner-Webb |

Rnd	Name	Pos	Ht	Wt	College

(Choice from Raiders in deal mentioned above)

| 5a | Terry Mickens (146) | WR | 6-0 | 200 | Florida A&M |
| 5b | Dorsey Levens (149) | RB | 6-1 | 235 | Georgia Tech |

(Choice from 49ers in deal mentioned above)

| 6a | Jay Kearney (169) | WR | 6-1 | 195 | West Virginia |

(Choice from Raiders in deal mentioned above)

| 6b | Ruffin Hamilton (175) | LB | 6-1 | 230 | Tulane |

(Choice from 49ers in deal mentioned above)

| 6c | Bill Schroeder (181) | WR | 6-1 | 195 | UW-La Crosse |
| 6d | Paul Duckworth (190) | LB | 6-1 | 245 | Connecticut |

(Choice from 49ers in deal mentioned above)

| 7 | **(Choice (212) to Broncos for Doug Widell)** | | | | |

When All-Pro receiver Sterling Sharpe suffered a career-ending injury late in the 1994 season, Favre emerged as the Packers undisputed leader.

1995

Team	Games	Att	Cmp	Yds	Cmp%	Y/Att	TD	Int	Rate
Green Bay	16	570	359	4,413	63.0	7.7	38	13	99.5

Favre Highlights

Favre was named MVP or Player of the Year by virtually every outlet, along with a variety of other Offensive Player of the Year awards and All-Pro selections. He became the third 4,000-yard passer in team history, with an NFL-best 4,413 passing yards, 45 yards shy of Lynn Dickey's team record. Had a streak of 17 straight games with a TD snapped late in the season and tied the NFL record with 12 straight games with at least two TD passes. Finished with 38 TD passes to lead the league. Favre began demonstrating his incredible toughness by playing through a severe ankle injury and, in a game against the Steelers, he was hit so hard that he coughed up blood during the ensuing timeout, then went back into the game and threw a TD pass.

CHRIS WILKINS/GETTY IMAGES

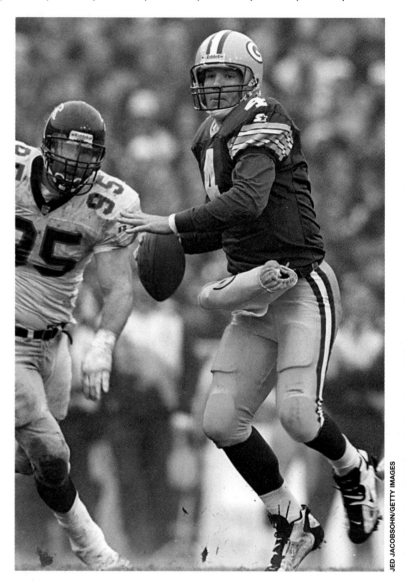

JED JACOBSOHN/GETTY IMAGES

Team Summary

Record: 11-5, Division Title.
Playoffs: Steamrolled the Falcons, 37-20, and 49ers, 27-17, before losing in NFC Championship at Dallas, 38-27.
Highlights: Won first divisional title since 1972. Edgar Bennett rushed for 1,067 yards while Robert Brooks had 102 catches for 1,497 yards and 13 TDs. Scored 30 or more points six times and won six of their last seven games to reach the playoffs.

GAME	DATE	OPPONENT	W/L	GB	Op.	LOCATION
1.	09-03-95	St. Louis Rams	Loss	14	17	Home
2.	09-11-95	Chicago Bears	Win	27	24	Away
3.	09-17-95	New York Giants	Win	14	6	Home
4.	09-24-95	Jacksonville Jaguars	Win	24	14	Away
5.	10-08-95	Dallas Cowboys	Loss	24	34	Away
6.	10-15-95	Detroit Lions	Win	30	21	Home
7.	10-22-95	Minnesota Vikings	Win	38	21	Home
8.	10-29-95	Detroit Lions	Loss	16	24	Away
9.	11-05-95	Minnesota Vikings	Loss	24	27	Away
10.	11-12-95	Chicago Bears	Win	35	28	Home
11.	11-19-95	Cleveland Browns	Win	31	20	Away
12.	11-26-95	Tampa Bay Buccaneers	Win	35	13	Home
13.	12-03-95	Cincinnati Bengals	Win	24	10	Home
14.	12-10-95	Tampa Bay Buccaneers	Loss	10	13	Away
15.	12-16-95	New Orleans Saints	Win	34	23	Away
16.	12-24-95	Pittsburgh Steelers	Win	24	19	Home
17.	12-31-95	Atlanta Falcons	Win	37	20	Home
18.	01-06-96	San Francisco 49ers	Win	27	17	Away
19.	01-14-96	Dallas Cowboys	Loss	27	38	Away

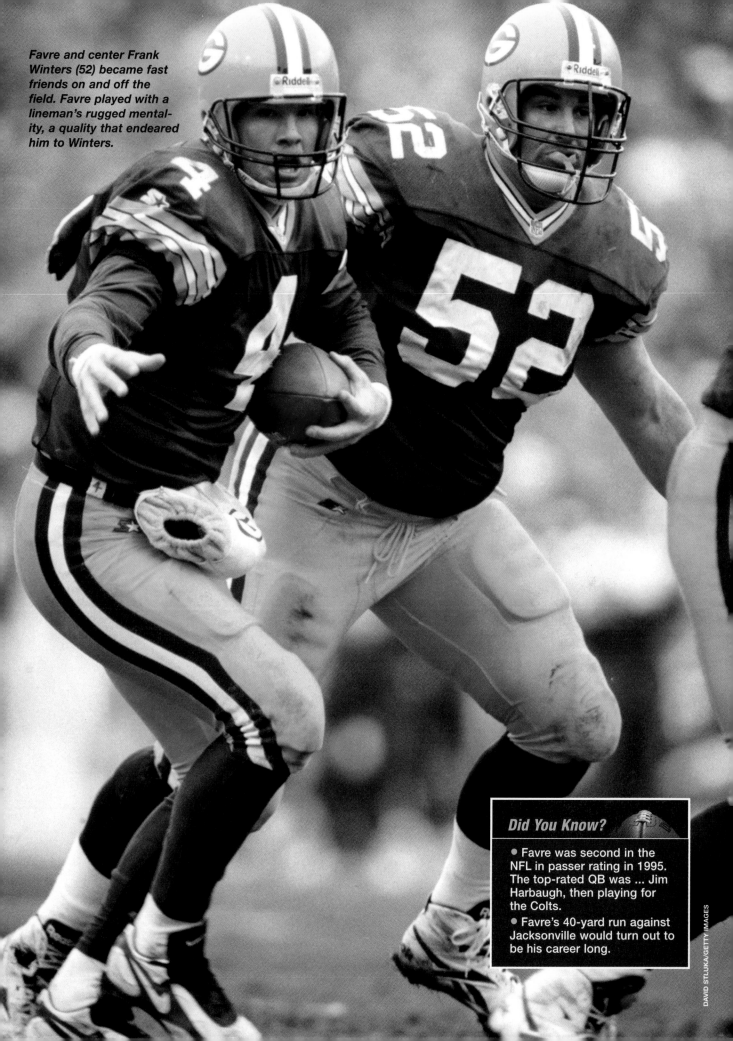

Favre and center Frank Winters (52) became fast friends on and off the field. Favre played with a lineman's rugged mentality, a quality that endeared him to Winters.

Did You Know?

• Favre was second in the NFL in passer rating in 1995. The top-rated QB was ... Jim Harbaugh, then playing for the Colts.

• Favre's 40-yard run against Jacksonville would turn out to be his career long.

TOM HAUCK/GETTY IMAGES

DAVID STLUKA/GETTY IMAGES

LC LARRY LAMBRECHT/NFL/GETTY IMAGES

ROSTER

No	Name	Pos	Ht	Wt	DOB	College	G
4	Favre, Brett	QB	6-2	220	10/10/69	Southern Mississippi	16
9	Borgognone, Dirk	K	6-2	221	01/09/68	Pacific	2
9	McMahon, Jim	QB	6-1	195	08/21/59	BYU	1
11	Detmer, Ty	QB	6-0	190	10/30/67	BYU	4
12	Rubley, T.J.	QB	6-3	205	11/29/68	Tulsa	1
13	Jacke, Chris	K	6-0	205	03/12/66	Texas-El Paso	14
17	Hentrich, Craig	P	6-3	200	05/18/71	Notre Dame	16
21	Newsome, Craig	CB	6-0	188	08/10/71	Arizona State	16
22	McGill, Lenny	CB	6-1	198	05/31/71	Arizona State	15
23	Dorsett, Matthew	CB	5-11	187	08/23/73	Southern	10
25	Levens, Dorsey	RB	6-1	240	05/21/70	Georgia Tech	15
28	Mullen, Roderick	CB	6-1	204	12/05/72	Grambling State	8
29	Wilson, Marcus	RB	6-1	215	04/16/68	Virginia	14
30	Henderson, William	FB	6-1	248	02/19/71	North Carolina	15
31	Teague, George	S	6-1	195	02/18/71	Alabama	15
32	Jervey, Travis	RB	5-11 1/2	225	05/05/72	The Citadel	16
33	Evans, Doug	CB	6-1	190	05/13/70	Louisiana Tech	16
34	Bennett, Edgar	RB	6-0	217	02/15/69	Florida State	16
36	Butler, LeRoy	S	6-0	200	07/19/68	Florida State	16
39	Prior, Mike	S	6-0	208	11/14/63	Illinois State	16
42	Johnson, LeShon	RB	5-11	200	01/15/71	Northern Illinois	2
45	Crawford, Keith	CB	6-2	198	11/21/70	Howard Payne	13
48	Bartrum, Mike	TE	6-4	245	06/23/70	Marshall	4
50	Arthur, Mike	C	6-3	280	05/07/68	Texas A&M	11
51	Williams, Brian	LB	6-1	240	12/17/72	USC	13
52	Winters, Frank	C	6-3	295	01/23/64	West Illinois	16
53	Koonce, George	LB	6-1	243	10/15/68	East Carolina	16
54	Harris, Bernardo	LB	6-2	243	10/15/71	North Carolina	11
55	Strickland, Fred	LB	6-2	250	08/15/66	Purdue	14
57	Kelly, Joe	LB	6-2	235	12/11/64	Washington	13
59	Simmons, Wayne	LB	6-2	248	12/15/69	Clemson	16
63	Timmerman, Adam	G	6-4	288	08/14/71	South Dakota State	13
64	Jurkovic, John	NT	6-2	295	08/18/67	Eastern Illinois	16
68	Sims, Joe	OL	6-3	310	03/01/69	Nebraska	4
71	Brown, Gary	T	6-4	315	06/25/71	Georgia Tech	16
72	Dotson, Earl	T	6-3	310	12/17/70	Texas A&I	16
73	Taylor, Aaron	G	6-4	305	11/14/72	Notre Dame	16
75	Ruettgers, Ken	T	6-5	292	08/20/62	USC	15
76	Galbreath, Harry	G	6-1	295	01/01/65	Tennessee	16
80	Jordan, Charles	WR	5-10	183	10/09/69	Long Beach City College	8
81	Morgan, Anthony	WR	6-1	200	11/15/67	Tennessee	16
82	Ingram, Mark	WR	5-11	194	08/23/65	Michigan State	16
83	Thomason, Jeff	TE	6-4	250	12/30/69	Oregon	16
83	Wilner, Jeff	TE	6-4	250	12/31/71	Wesleyan	2
85	Mickens, Terry	WR	6-0	198	02/21/71	Florida A&M	16
86	Freeman, Antonio	WR	6-0 1/2	187	05/27/72	Virginia Tech	11
87	Brooks, Robert	WR	6-0	180	06/23/70	South Carolina	16
88	Jackson, Keith	TE	6-2	258	04/19/65	Oklahoma	9
89	Chmura, Mark	TE	6-5	250	02/22/69	Boston College	16
90	Holland, Darius	DT	6-4	305	11/10/73	Colorado	14
91	Clavelle, Shannon	DE	6-2	287	10/12/72	Colorado	1
92	White, Reggie	DE	6-5	300	12/19/61	Tennessee	15
93	Brown, Gilbert	NT	6-2	325	02/22/71	Kansas	13
94	Kuberski, Bob	NT	6-4	300	04/05/71	Navy	9
96	Jones, Sean	DE	6-7	283	12/19/62	Northeastern	16
97	LaBounty, Matt	DE	6-3	278	01/03/69	Oregon	14
98	Wilkins, Gabe	DE	6-4	300	09/01/71	Gardner-Webb	13

DRAFT

Rnd	Name	Pos	Ht	Wt	College
1a	(Packers traded 1st-round pick (22) and 6th-round pick (188) to Panthers for Panthers' 1st-round (32), 3rd-round (65), and 6th-round (173) picks)				
1b	Craig Newsome (32) (Choice from Panthers in deal mentioned above)	DB	6-0	185	Arizona State
2	(Choice (53) traded to Dolphins for Keith Jackson)				
3a	Darius Holland (65) (Choice from Panthers in deal mentioned above)	DT	6-4	310	Colorado
3b	William Henderson (66) (Choice from Jaguars for Mark Brunell)	FB	6-1	246	North Carolina
3c	Brian Williams (73) (Compensation from Seahawks for Corey Harris)	LB	6-1	238	USC
3d	(Choice (84) to Browns for Browns' 3rd-rd (90) and 5th-rd (160) picks)				
3e	Antonio Freeman (90) (Choice from Browns in deal mentioned above)	WR	6-0 1/2	185	Virginia Tech
4	Jeff Miller (117)	T	6-3	303	Mississippi
5a	Jay Barker (160) (Choice from Browns in deal mentioned above)	QB	6-2	212	Alabama
5b	Travis Jervey (170) (Choice to Raiders for Charles Jordan; from Jaguars for Mark Brunell)	RB	5-11 1/2	210	The Citadel
6a	Charlie Simmons (173) (Choice from Panthers in deal mentioned above)	WR	6-3	202	Georgia Tech
6b	(Choice (188) to Panthers in deal mentioned above)				
7	Adam Timmerman (230)	G	6-4	289	So. Dakota State

Favre led the Packers to 11 victories in 1995, Green Bays' first 11-win season in 29 years.

By The Numbers...

99 Favre's TD pass to Robert Brooks on Sept. 11 was the eighth such score in league history.

8 Favre threw eight TD passes in three postseason games.

10 Favre won 10 different MVP or Player of the Year awards from organizations and publications throughout the country in 1995.

1996

Team	Games	Att	Cmp	Yds	Cmp%	Y/Att	TD	Int	Rate
Green Bay	16	543	325	3,899	59.9	7.2	39	13	95.8

Favre Highlights

In the Packers' Super Bowl victory over New England, Favre threw a TD pass to Andre Rison on the first series, calling a famous audible and, after the score, removing his helmet and racing off the field for probably his most memorabile career moment. Also audibled for an 81-yard TD pass to Antonio Freeman, the longest in Super Bowl history. Favre accounted for one other score with a rare rushing TD. Again, won too many MVP and Player of the Year awards to list. His 39 TD passes broke his own team record and at the time set an NFC record. Led the NFC with 3,899 yards passing.

ANDY HAYT/GETTY IMAGES

AL BELLO/GETTY IMAGES

Team Summary

Record: 13-3, Division Title.
Playoffs: Won first Super Bowl in 29 years, 35-21, over New England at the New Orleans Superdome.
Highlights: Had the top-ranked offense and defense, the first team since the undefeated Dolphins in 1972 to accomplish that feat. Edgar Bennett and Dorsey Levens teamed to combine for more than 1,400 yards rushing while Antonio Freeman had 933 yards receiving and nine TDs in only 12 games.

GETTY IMAGES

GAME	DATE	OPPONENT	W/L	GB	Op.	LOCATION
1.	09-01-96	Tampa Bay Buccaneers	Win	34	3	Away
2.	09-09-96	Philadelphia Eagles	Win	39	13	Home
3.	09-15-96	San Diego Chargers	Win	42	10	Home
4.	09-22-96	Minnesota Vikings	Loss	21	30	Away
5.	09-29-96	Seattle Seahawks	Win	31	10	Away
6.	10-06-96	Chicago Bears	Win	37	6	Away
7.	10-14-96	San Francisco 49ers	Win	23	20	Home
8.	10-27-96	Tampa Bay Buccaneers	Win	13	7	Home
9.	11-03-96	Detroit Lions	Win	28	18	Home
10.	11-10-96	Kansas City Chiefs	Loss	20	27	Away
11.	11-18-96	Dallas Cowboys	Loss	6	21	Away
12.	11-24-96	St. Louis Rams	Win	24	9	Away
13.	12-01-96	Chicago Bears	Win	28	17	Home
14.	12-08-96	Denver Broncos	Win	41	6	Home
15.	12-15-96	Detroit Lions	Win	31	3	Away
16.	12-22-96	Minnesota Vikings	Win	38	10	Home
17.	01-04-97	San Francisco 49ers	Win	35	14	Home
18.	01-12-97	Carolina Panthers	Win	30	13	Home
Super Bowl XXXI						
19.	01-26-97	New England Patriots	Win	35	21	New Orleans

Favre threw touchdown passes to 10 different teammates in 1996, including a team-best 80-yard pass to Don Beebe.

Did You Know?

• Favre helped the Packers' defense finish No. 1 in the NFL by shredding the Denver defense that going into the Dec. 8 game had been rated No. 1. Favre threw four TD passes that day.

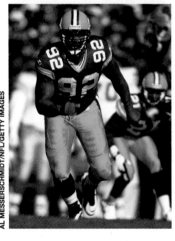

ROSTER

No	Name	Pos	Ht	Wt	DOB	College	G
4	Favre, Brett	QB	6-2	225	10/10/69	Southern Mississippi	16
9	McMahon, Jim	QB	6-1	195	08/21/59	BYU	5
13	Jacke, Chris	K	6-0	205	03/12/66	Texas-El Paso	16
17	Hentrich, Craig	P	6-3	200	05/18/71	Notre Dame	16
18	Pederson, Doug	QB	6-3	215	01/31/68	Northeast Louisiana	1
21	Newsome, Craig	CB	6-0	190	08/10/71	Arizona State	16
22	Brooks, Bucky	CB	6-0	195	01/22/71	North Carolina	2
25	Levens, Dorsey	RB	6-1	235	05/21/70	Georgia Tech	16
27	Jones, Calvin	RB	5-11	205	11/27/70	Nebraska	1
28	Mullen, Roderick	CB	6-1	204	12/05/72	Grambling State	14
30	Henderson, William	FB	6-1	248	02/19/71	North Carolina	16
32	Jervey, Travis	RB	5-11 1/2	225	05/05/72	The Citadel	16
33	Evans, Doug	CB	6-1	190	05/13/70	Louisiana Tech	16
34	Bennett, Edgar	RB	6-0	217	02/15/69	Florida State	16
36	Butler, LeRoy	S	6-0	200	07/19/68	Florida State	16
37	Williams, Tyrone	CB	5-11	195	05/31/73	Nebraska	16
38	Satterfield, Brian	FB	6-0	225	12/22/69	North Alabama	1
39	Prior, Mike	S	6-0	208	11/14/63	Illinois State	16
40	Hayes, Chris	S	6-0	200	05/07/72	Washington State	2
41	Robinson, Eugene	S	6-0	195	05/28/63	Colgate	16
42	Dowden, Corey	CB	5-11	190	10/18/68	Tulane	9
46	Robinson, Michael	CB	6-1	192	06/24/73	Hampton	6
49	Smith, Kevin	TE	6-4	255	07/25/69	UCLA	1
50	Arthur, Mike	C	6-3	280	05/07/68	Texas A&M	5
51	Williams, Brian	LB	6-1	235	12/17/72	USC	16
52	Winters, Frank	C	6-3	295	01/23/64	West Illinois	16
53	Koonce, George	LB	6-1	243	10/15/68	East Carolina	16
54	Cox, Ron	LB	6-2	235	03/29/68	Fresno State	16
55	Harris, Bernardo	LB	6-2	243	10/15/71	North Carolina	16
56	Hollinquest, Lamont	LB	6-3	243	10/24/70	USC	16
59	Simmons, Wayne	LB	6-2	248	12/15/69	Clemson	16
60	McGuire, Gene	C	6-2	285	07/17/70	Notre Dame	8
63	Timmerman, Adam	G	6-4	295	08/14/71	South Dakota State	16
64	Wilkerson, Bruce	T	6-5	305	07/28/64	Tennessee	14
65	Knapp, Lindsey	G	6-6	300	02/25/70	Notre Dame	9
67	Dellenbach, Jeff	C	6-6	300	02/14/63	Wisconsin	3
68	Brown, Gary	T	6-4	315	06/25/71	Georgia Tech	8
71	Dotson, Santana	DT	6-5	285	12/19/69	Baylor	16
72	Dotson, Earl	T	6-3	315	12/17/70	Texas A&I	15
73	Taylor, Aaron	G	6-4	305	11/14/72	Notre Dame	16
75	Ruettgers, Ken	T	6-5	292	08/20/62	USC	4
77	Michels, John	T	6-7	290	03/19/73	USC	15
80	Mayes, Derrick	WR	6-0	200	01/28/74	Notre Dame	7
81	Howard, Desmond	WR	5-10	180	05/15/70	Michigan	16
81	Morgan, Anthony	WR	6-1	200	11/15/67	Tennessee	3
82	Beebe, Don	WR	5-11	183	12/18/64	Chadron State	16
83	Thomason, Jeff	TE	6-4	250	12/30/69	Oregon	16
84	Rison, Andre	WR	6-1	195	03/18/67	Michigan State	5
85	Mickens, Terry	WR	6-0	198	02/21/71	Florida A&M	8
86	Freeman, Antonio	WR	6-0 1/2	190	05/27/72	Virginia Tech	12
87	Brooks, Robert	WR	6-0	180	06/23/70	South Carolina	7
88	Jackson, Keith	TE	6-2	258	04/19/65	Oklahoma	16
89	Chmura, Mark	TE	6-5	250	02/22/69	Boston College	13
90	Holland, Darius	DT	6-4	310	11/10/73	Colorado	16
91	Clavelle, Shannon	DE	6-2	287	10/12/72	Colorado	8
92	White, Reggie	DE	6-5	300	12/19/61	Tennessee	16
93	Brown, Gilbert	NT	6-2	325	02/22/71	Kansas	16
94	Kuberski, Bob	NT	6-4	295	04/05/71	Navy	1
95	McKenzie, Keith	DE	6-3	242	10/17/73	Ball State	10
96	Jones, Sean	DE	6-7	283	12/19/62	Northeastern	15
98	Wilkins, Gabe	DE	6-4	305	09/01/71	Gardner-Webb	16

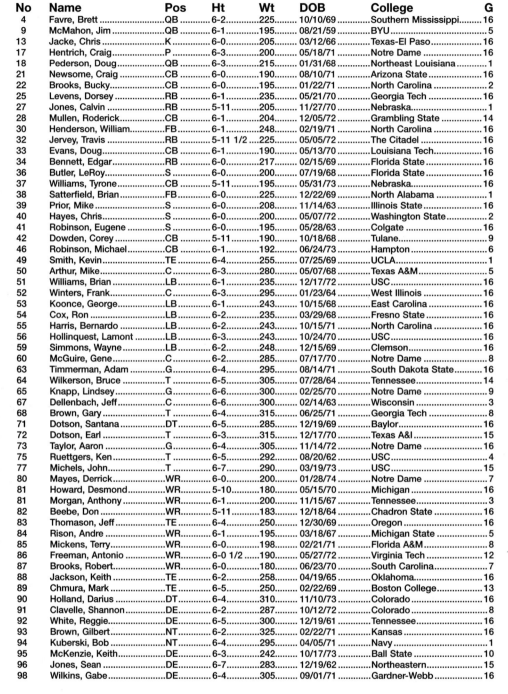

DRAFT

Rnd	Name	Pos	Ht	Wt	College
1	John Michels (27)	T	6-7	282	USC
2	Derrick Mayes (56)	WR	6-0	204	Notre Dame
3a	Mike Flanagan (90)	C	6-5	290	UCLA
3b	Tyrone Williams (93)	DB	5-11	195	Nebraska
	(Free agent compensatory pick)				
4	Chris Darkins (123)	RB	6-0	215	Minnesota
5	(Choice (161) to Chiefs for Lindsay Knapp)				

Rnd	Name	Pos	Ht	Wt	College
6a	(Choice (197) to Eagles for Joe Sims)				
6b	Marco Rivera (208)	G	6-4	295	Penn State
	(Free agent compensatory pick)				
7a	Kyle Wachholtz (240)	QB	6-4	235	USC
7b	Keith McKenzie (252)	LB	6-3	238	Ball State
	(Free agent compensatory pick)				

FRONT ROW: (L-R) 4 Brett Favre, 9 Jim McMahon, 13 Chris Jacke, 17 Craig Hentrich, 18 Doug Pederson, 21 Craig Newsome, 25 Dorsey Levens, 28 Roderick Mullen, 30 William Henderson, 32 Travis Jervey.

SECOND ROW: (L-R) Tight Ends/Assistant Offensive Line Coach Andy Reid, Offensive Line Coach Tom Lovat, Quarterbacks Coach Marty Mornhinweg, Running Backs Coach Harry Sydney, Wide Receivers Coach Gil Haskell, Offensive Coordinator Sherman Lewis, Head Coach Mike Holmgren, Defensive Coordinator Fritz Shurmur, Defensive Line Coach Larry Brooks, Linebackers Coach Jim Lind, Defensive Assistant/Quality Control Johnny Holland, Defensive Backs Coach Bob Valesente, Strength and Conditioning Coach Kent Johnston, Special Teams Coach Nolan Cromwell.

THIRD ROW: (L-R) 33 Doug Evans, 34 Edgar Bennett, 36 LeRoy Butler, 37 Tyrone Williams, 39 Mike Prior, 41 Eugene Robinson, 42 Corey Dowden, 49 Kevin Smith, 50 Mike Arthur, 51 Brian Williams, 52 Frank Winters.

FOURTH ROW: (L-R) 53 George Koonce, 54 Ron Cox, 55 Bernardo Harris, 56 Lamont Hollinquest, 59 Wayne Simmons, 62 Marco Rivera, 63 Adam Timmerman, 64 Bruce Wilkerson, 65 Lindsay Knapp, 68 Gary Brown.

FIFTH ROW: (L-R) 71 Santana Dotson, 72 Earl Dotson, 73 Aaron Taylor, 75 Ken Ruettgers, 77 John Michels, 80 Derrick Mayes, 81 Desmond Howard, 82 Don Beebe, 83 Jeff Thomason, 85 Terry Mickens, 86 Antonio Freeman.

SIXTH ROW: (L-R) 87 Robert Brooks, 88 Keith Jackson, 89 Mark Chmura, 90 Darius Holland, 91 Shannon Clavelle, 92 Reggie White, 93 Gilbert Brown, 94 Bob Kuberski, 95 Keith McKenzie, 96 Sean Jones, 98 Gabe Wilkins.

BACK ROW: (L-R) Strength and Conditioning Assistant Barry Rubin, Offensive Assistant/Quality Control Gary Reynolds, Corporate Security Officer Jerry Parins, Training Room Intern Andre Daniel, Assistant Trainer Sam Ramsden, Assistant Trainer Kurt Fielding, Head Trainer Pepper Burruss, Associate Team Physician Dr. John Gray, Team Physician Dr. Patrick J. McKenzie, Equipment Manager Gordon (Red) Batty, Assistant Equipment Manager Bryan Nehring, Assistant Equipment Manager Tom Bakken, Equipment Assistant Tim O'Neill, Video Assistant Chris Kirby, Assistant Video Director Bob Eckberg, Video Director Al Treml.

1997

Team	Games	Att	Cmp	Yds	Cmp%	Y/Att	TD	Int	Rate
Green Bay	16	513	304	3,867	59.3	7.5	35	16	92.6

Favre Highlights

Shared Associated Press MVP honors with Barry Sanders to become the first NFL player to win three straight MVP awards. Had 3,867 yards and 35 TDs. Enjoyed a huge statistical day in a loss against the Colts, with 363 yards passing and three scores as the Packers scored on their first six possessions. Beat the nemesis Cowboys 45-17 with four TD passes and had a season-high five TDs in a win against Minnesota.

DOUG PENSINGER/GETTY IMAGES

JEFF HAYNES/GETTY IMAGES

Team Summary

Record: 13-3, Division Title
Playoffs: Reached Super Bowl for second straight year but a depleted defense couldn't stop Denver RB Terrell Davis in a 31-24 loss. It was the team's first loss in a Super Bowl after three straight wins.
Highlights: Dorsey Levens had 1,435 yards rushing, second in team history to Jim Taylor's 1,474 (Taylor's was in 14 games, of course.) Both Antonio Freeman and Robert Brooks reached 1,000 yards receiving.

GETTY IMAGES

GAME	DATE	OPPONENT	W/L	GB	Op.	LOCATION
1.	09-01-97	Chicago Bears	Win	38	24	Home
2.	09-07-97	Philadelphia Eagles	Loss	9	10	Away
3.	09-14-97	Miami Dolphins	Win	23	18	Home
4.	09-21-97	Minnesota Vikings	Win	38	32	Home
5.	09-28-97	Detroit Lions	Loss	15	26	Away
6.	10-05-97	Tampa Bay Buccaneers	Win	21	16	Home
7.	10-12-97	Chicago Bears	Win	24	23	Away
8.	10-27-97	New England Patriots	Win	28	10	Away
9.	11-02-97	Detroit Lions	Win	20	10	Home
10.	11-09-97	St. Louis Rams	Win	17	7	Home
11.	11-16-97	Indianapolis Colts	Loss	38	41	Away
12.	11-23-97	Dallas Cowboys	Win	45	17	Home
13.	12-01-97	Minnesota Vikings	Win	27	11	Away
14.	12-07-97	Tampa Bay Buccaneers	Win	17	6	Away
15.	12-14-97	Carolina Panthers	Win	31	10	Away
16.	12-20-97	Buffalo Bills	Win	31	21	Home
17.	01-04-98	Tampa Bay Buccaneers	Win	21	7	Away
18.	01-11-98	San Francisco 49ers	Win	23	10	Away
	Super Bowl XXXII					
19.	01-25-98	Denver Broncos	Loss	24	31	San Diego

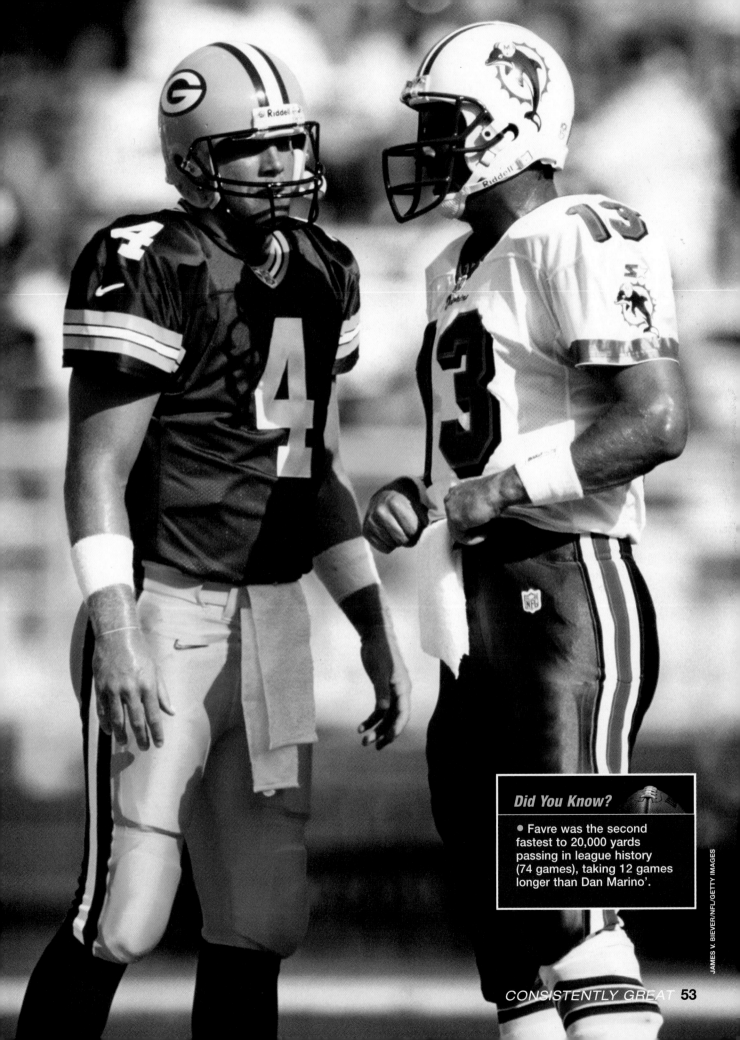

Did You Know?

● Favre was the second fastest to 20,000 yards passing in league history (74 games), taking 12 games longer than Dan Marino'.

ROSTER

DAVID STLUKA/GETTY IMAGES

DAVID STLUKA/GETTY IMAGES

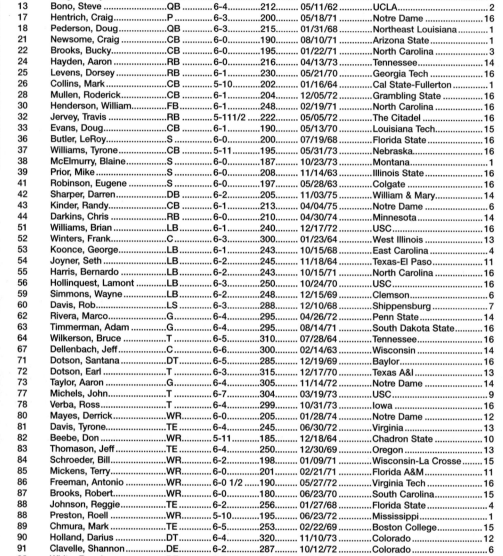

BRIAN BAHR/GETTY IMAGES

No	Name	Pos	Ht	Wt	DOB	College	G
4	Favre, Brett	QB	6-2	225	10/10/69	Southern Mississippi	16
8	Longwell, Ryan	K	6-0	185	08/16/74	California	16
13	Bono, Steve	QB	6-4	212	05/11/62	UCLA	2
17	Hentrich, Craig	P	6-3	200	05/18/71	Notre Dame	16
18	Pederson, Doug	QB	6-3	215	01/31/68	Northeast Louisiana	1
21	Newsome, Craig	CB	6-0	190	08/10/71	Arizona State	1
22	Brooks, Bucky	CB	6-0	195	01/22/71	North Carolina	3
24	Hayden, Aaron	RB	6-0	216	04/13/73	Tennessee	14
25	Levens, Dorsey	RB	6-1	230	05/21/70	Georgia Tech	16
26	Collins, Mark	CB	5-10	202	01/16/64	Cal State-Fullerton	1
28	Mullen, Roderick	CB	6-1	204	12/05/72	Grambling State	16
30	Henderson, William	FB	6-1	248	02/19/71	North Carolina	16
32	Jervey, Travis	RB	5-11 1/2	222	05/05/72	The Citadel	16
33	Evans, Doug	CB	6-1	190	05/13/70	Louisiana Tech	15
36	Butler, LeRoy	S	6-0	200	07/19/68	Florida State	16
37	Williams, Tyrone	CB	5-11	195	05/31/73	Nebraska	16
38	McElmurry, Blaine	S	6-0	187	10/23/73	Montana	1
39	Prior, Mike	S	6-0	208	11/14/63	Illinois State	16
41	Robinson, Eugene	S	6-0	197	05/28/63	Colgate	16
42	Sharper, Darren	DB	6-2	205	11/03/75	William & Mary	14
43	Kinder, Randy	CB	6-1	213	04/04/75	Notre Dame	6
44	Darkins, Chris	RB	6-0	210	04/30/74	Minnesota	14
51	Williams, Brian	LB	6-1	240	12/17/72	USC	16
52	Winters, Frank	C	6-3	300	01/23/64	West Illinois	13
53	Koonce, George	LB	6-1	243	10/15/68	East Carolina	4
54	Joyner, Seth	LB	6-2	245	11/18/64	Texas-El Paso	11
55	Harris, Bernardo	LB	6-2	243	10/15/71	North Carolina	16
56	Hollinquest, Lamont	LB	6-3	250	10/24/70	USC	16
59	Simmons, Wayne	LB	6-2	248	12/15/69	Clemson	6
60	Davis, Rob	LS	6-3	288	12/10/68	Shippensburg	7
62	Rivera, Marco	G	6-4	295	04/26/72	Penn State	14
63	Timmerman, Adam	G	6-4	295	08/14/71	South Dakota State	16
64	Wilkerson, Bruce	T	6-5	310	07/28/64	Tennessee	16
67	Dellenbach, Jeff	C	6-6	300	02/14/63	Wisconsin	14
71	Dotson, Santana	DT	6-5	285	12/19/69	Baylor	16
72	Dotson, Earl	T	6-3	315	12/17/70	Texas A&I	13
73	Taylor, Aaron	G	6-4	305	11/14/72	Notre Dame	14
77	Michels, John	T	6-7	304	03/19/73	USC	9
78	Verba, Ross	T	6-4	299	10/31/73	Iowa	16
80	Mayes, Derrick	WR	6-0	205	01/28/74	Notre Dame	12
81	Davis, Tyrone	TE	6-4	245	06/30/72	Virginia	13
82	Beebe, Don	WR	5-11	185	12/18/64	Chadron State	10
83	Thomason, Jeff	TE	6-4	250	12/30/69	Oregon	13
84	Schroeder, Bill	WR	6-2	198	01/09/71	Wisconsin-La Crosse	15
85	Mickens, Terry	WR	6-0	201	02/21/71	Florida A&M	11
86	Freeman, Antonio	WR	6-0 1/2	190	05/27/72	Virginia Tech	16
87	Brooks, Robert	WR	6-0	180	06/23/70	South Carolina	15
88	Johnson, Reggie	TE	6-2	256	01/27/68	Florida State	4
88	Preston, Roell	WR	5-10	195	06/23/72	Mississippi	1
89	Chmura, Mark	TE	6-5	253	02/22/69	Boston College	15
90	Holland, Darius	DT	6-4	320	11/10/73	Colorado	12
91	Clavelle, Shannon	DE	6-2	287	10/12/72	Colorado	6
92	White, Reggie	DE	6-5	304	12/19/61	Tennessee	16
93	Brown, Gilbert	NT	6-2	345	02/22/71	Kansas	12
94	Kuberski, Bob	NT	6-4	295	04/05/71	Navy	11
95	McKenzie, Keith	DE	6-3	255	10/17/73	Ball State	16
96	Williams, Gerald	DL	6-3	290	09/08/63	Auburn	4
97	Frase, Paul	DE	6-5	267	05/06/65	Syracuse	8
98	Wilkins, Gabe	DE	6-4	295	09/01/71	Gardner-Webb	16
99	Smith, Jermaine	DT	6-3	289	02/03/72	Georgia	9

DRAFT

Rnd	Name	Pos	Ht	Wt	College
1	Ross Verba (30)	T	6-4	299	Iowa
2	Darren Sharper (60)	DB	6-2	205	William & Mary
3	Brett Conway (90)	K	6-2	192	Penn State
4	Jermaine Smith (126)	DT	6-3	290	Georgia
5	Anthony Hicks (160)	LB	6-1	242	Arkansas
6	(Choice (193) to Raiders for Raiders' 7th-round pick (213))				

Rnd	Name	Pos	Ht	Wt	College
7a	Chris Miller (213)	WR	5-10	192	USC
	(Choice from Raiders in deal mentioned above)				
7b	Jerald Sowell (231)	RB	6-0	246	Tulane
7c	Ronnie McAda (240)	QB	6-3	202	Army
	(Free agent compensatory pick)				

1997 GREEN BAY PACKERS

FRONT ROW: (L-R) 4 Brett Favre, 8 Ryan Longwell, 10 Brett Conway, 13 Steve Bono, 17 Craig Hentrich, 18 Doug Pederson, 21 Craig Newsome, 24 Aaron Hayden, 25 Dorsey Levens, 28 Roderick Mullen, 30 William Henderson.

SECOND ROW: (L-R) Special Teams Coach Nolan Cromwell, Quarterbacks Coach Andy Reid, Tight Ends/Assistant Offensive Line Coach Mike Sherman, Offensive Line Coach Tom Lovat, Running Backs Coach Harry Sydney, Wide Receivers Coach Gil Haskell, Offensive Coordinator Sherman Lewis, Head Coach Mike Holmgren, Defensive Coordinator Fritz Shurmur, Defensive Line Coach Larry Brooks, Linebackers Coach Jim Lind, Defensive Assistant/Quality Control Johnny Holland, Defensive Backs Coach Bob Valesente, Strength and Conditioning Coach Kent Johnston, Strength and Conditioning Assistant Barry Rubin.

THIRD ROW: (L-R) 32 Travis Jervey, 33 Doug Evans, 34 Edgar Bennett, 36 LeRoy Butler, 37 Tyrone Williams, 39 Mike Prior, 41 Eugene Robinson, 42 Darren Sharper, 44 Chris Darkins, 50 Anthony Hicks, 51 Brian Williams, 52 Frank Winters.

FOURTH ROW: (L-R) 53 George Koonce, 54 Seth Joyner, 55 Bernardo Harris, 56 Lamont Hollinquest, 58 Mike Flanagan, 59 Wayne Simmons, 62 Marco Rivera, 63 Adam Timmerman, 64 Bruce Wilkerson, 67 Jeff Dellenbach, 70 Joe Andruzzi.

FIFTH ROW: (L-R) 71 Santana Dotson, 72 Earl Dotson, 73 Aaron Taylor, 77 John Michels, 78 Ross Verba, 80 Derrick Mayes, 81 Tyrone Davis, 82 Don Beebe, 83 Jeff Thomason, 84 Bill Schroeder, 85 Terry Mickens, 86 Antonio Freeman.

SIXTH ROW: (L-R) 87 Robert Brooks, 89 Mark Chmura, 90 Darius Holland, 91 Shannon Clavelle, 92 Reggie White, 93 Gilbert Brown, 94 Bob Kuberski, 95 Keith McKenzie, 97 Paul Frase, 98 Gabe Wilkins, 99 Jermaine Smith.

BACK ROW: (L-R) Administrative Assistant/Football Bill Nayes, Offensive Assistant/Quality Control Gary Reynolds, Corporate Security Officer Jerry Parins, Training Room Intern Bryan Engle, Assistant Trainer Sam Ramsden, Assistant Trainer Kurt Fielding, Head Trainer Pepper Burruss, Associate Team Physician Dr. John Gray, Team Physician Dr. Patrick J. McKenzie, Equipment Manager Gordon (Red) Batty, Assistant Equipment Manager Bryan Nehring, Assistant Equipment Manager Tom Bakken, Equipment Assistant Tim O'Neill, Video Assistant Chris Kirby, Assistant Video Director Bob Eckberg, Video Director Al Treml.

1998

Team	Games	Att	Cmp	Yds	Cmp%	Y/Att	TD	Int	Rate
Green Bay	16	551	347	4,212	63.0	7.6	31	23	87.8

Favre Highlights

Led the NFL in passing yards with 4,212 and led the league in completion percentage. Although his 87.8 rating was down a bit, he did have 31 TD passes. Had five TD passes and 388 yards passing against Carolina. Rushed for 49 yards in a game against the Tennessee Oilers.

PETER MUHLY/GETTY IMAGES

VINCENT LAFORET/AFP/GETTY IMAGES

Team Summary

Record: 11-5, Wild Card

Playoffs: Lost 30-27 in Mike Holmgren's last game as head coach on the game-ending Terrell Owens TD catch at San Francisco in the first round of the playoffs.

Highlights: Dorsey Levens got hurt and Darick Holmes led the team with only 386 yards rushing. Antonio Freeman had 84 catches for 1,424 yards and 14 TDs. Reggie White had 16 sacks and was named the NFL's Defensive Player of the Year.

GAME	DATE	OPPONENT	W/L	GB	Op.	LOCATION
1.	09-06-98	Detroit Lions	Win	38	19	Home
2.	09-13-98	Tampa Bay Buccaneers	Win	23	15	Home
3.	09-20-98	Cincinnati Bengals	Win	13	6	Away
4.	09-27-98	Carolina Panthers	Win	37	30	Away
5.	10-05-98	Minnesota Vikings	Loss	24	37	Home
6.	10-15-98	Detroit Lions	Loss	20	27	Away
7.	10-25-98	Baltimore Ravens	Win	28	10	Home
8.	11-01-98	San Francisco 49ers	Win	36	22	Home
9.	11-09-98	Pittsburgh Steelers	Loss	20	27	Away
10.	11-15-98	New York Giants	Win	37	3	Away
11.	11-22-98	Minnesota Vikings	Loss	14	28	Away
12.	11-29-98	Philadelphia Eagles	Win	24	16	Home
13.	12-07-98	Tampa Bay Buccaneers	Loss	22	24	Away
14.	12-13-98	Chicago Bears	Win	26	20	Home
15.	12-20-98	Tennessee Oilers	Win	30	22	Home
16.	12-27-98	Chicago Bears	Win	16	13	Away
17.	01-03-99	San Francisco 49ers	Loss	27	30	Away

By The Numbers...

10 Favre threw a TD pass in a club-record 10th straight postseason game, the disappointing loss at San Francisco.

A last-second touchdown pass from Steve Young to Terrell Owens ended the Packers' 1998 playoff hopes, 30-27. It also ended Coach Mike Holmgren's career in Green Bay: Holmgren resigned five days later to join the Seattle Seahawks.

1998

GRANT HALVERSON/AFP/GETTY IMAGES

JONATHAN DANIEL/GETTY IMAGES

ALLEN KEE/NFL/GETTY IMAGES

ROSTER

No	Name	Pos	Ht	Wt	DOB	College	G
4	Favre, Brett	QB	6-2	230	10/10/69	Southern Mississippi	16
7	Landeta, Sean	P	6-0	200	01/06/62	Towson State	16
8	Longwell, Ryan	K	6-0	192	08/16/74	California	16
16	Copeland, Russell	WR	6-0	200	11/04/71	Memphis State	3
18	Pederson, Doug	QB	6-3	215	01/31/68	Northeast Louisiana	12
21	Newsome, Craig	CB	6-0	190	08/10/71	Arizona State	13
22	Holmes, Darick	RB	6-0	226	07/01/71	Portland State	11
23	Blackmon, Roosevelt	CB	6-1	185	09/10/74	Morris Brown	3
25	Levens, Dorsey	RB	6-1	228	05/21/70	Georgia Tech	7
27	Blair, Michael	RB	5-11	245	11/26/74	Ball State	11
29	Harris, Raymont	RB	6-0	225	06/13/69	Ohio State	8
31	Smith, Rod	CB	5-11	187	03/12/70	Notre Dame	8
32	Jervey, Travis	RB	5-11 1/2	222	05/05/72	The Citadel	8
33	Henderson, William	FB	6-1	245	02/19/71	North Carolina	16
36	Butler, LeRoy	S	6-0	198	07/19/68	Florida State	16
37	Williams, Tyrone	CB	5-11	192	05/31/73	Nebraska	16
39	Prior, Mike	S	6-0	208	11/14/63	Illinois State	16
40	Terrell, Pat	S	6-1	208	03/18/68	Notre Dame	16
42	Sharper, Darren	DB	6-2	210	11/03/75	William & Mary	16
43	McGarrahan, Scott	S	6-1	197	02/12/74	New Mexico	15
45	Cooks, Kerry	S	5-11	202	03/28/74	Iowa	9
46	Bolden, Juran	CB	6-2	201	06/27/74	Miss. Delta Community	3
47	Galbraith, Scott	TE	6-2	254	01/07/67	USC	1
48	Kitts, Jim	FB	6-1	245	12/28/72	Ferrum	2
51	Williams, Brian	LB	6-1	245	12/17/72	USC	16
52	Winters, Frank	C	6-3	300	01/23/64	West Illinois	13
53	Koonce, George	LB	6-1	245	10/15/68	East Carolina	14
54	Waddy, Jude	LB	6-2	220	09/12/75	William & Mary	14
55	Harris, Bernardo	LB	6-2	248	10/15/71	North Carolina	16
56	Hollinquest, Lamont	LB	6-3	250	10/24/70	USC	14
57	London, Antonio	LB	6-2	238	04/14/71	Alabama	1
58	Flanagan, Mike	C	6-5	290	11/10/73	UCLA	2
60	Davis, Rob	LS	6-3	290	12/10/68	Shippensburg	16
62	Rivera, Marco	G	6-4	305	04/26/72	Penn State	15
63	Timmerman, Adam	G	6-4	300	08/14/71	South Dakota State	16
67	Dellenbach, Jeff	C	6-6	300	02/14/63	Wisconsin	16
68	Wahle, Mike	G	6-6	306	03/29/77	Navy	1
70	Andruzzi, Joe	G	6-3	310	08/23/75	S.Connecticut State	15
71	Dotson, Santana	DT	6-5	285	12/19/69	Baylor	16
72	Dotson, Earl	T	6-3	315	12/17/70	Texas A&I	16
76	Willig, Matt	T	6-7	315	01/21/69	USC	16
78	Verba, Ross	T	6-4	302	10/31/73	Iowa	16
80	Mayes, Derrick	WR	6-0	205	01/28/74	Notre Dame	10
81	Davis, Tyrone	TE	6-4	252	06/30/72	Virginia	13
82	Manning, Brian	WR	5-11	186	04/22/75	Stanford	3
83	Thomason, Jeff	TE	6-4	255	12/30/69	Oregon	16
84	Schroeder, Bill	WR	6-2	198	01/09/71	Wisconsin-La Crosse	13
85	Bradford, Corey	WR	6-1	197	12/08/75	Jackson State	8
86	Freeman, Antonio	WR	6-0 1/2	198	05/27/72	Virginia Tech	15
87	Brooks, Robert	WR	6-0	180	06/23/70	South Carolina	12
88	Preston, Roell	WR	5-10	195	06/23/72	Mississippi	16
89	Chmura, Mark	TE	6-5	255	02/22/69	Boston College	15
90	Holliday, Vonnie	DE	6-5	296	12/11/75	North Carolina	12
91	Brown, Jonathan	DE	6-4	265	11/28/75	Tennessee	4
92	White, Reggie	DE	6-5	300	12/19/61	Tennessee	16
93	Brown, Gilbert	NT	6-2	350	02/22/71	Kansas	16
94	Kuberski, Bob	NT	6-4	298	04/05/71	Navy	16
95	McKenzie, Keith	DE	6-3	264	10/17/73	Ball State	16
96	Booker, Vaughn	DE/DT	6-5	300	02/24/68	Cincinnati	16
98	Lyon, Billy	DT	6-5	295	12/10/73	Marshall	4

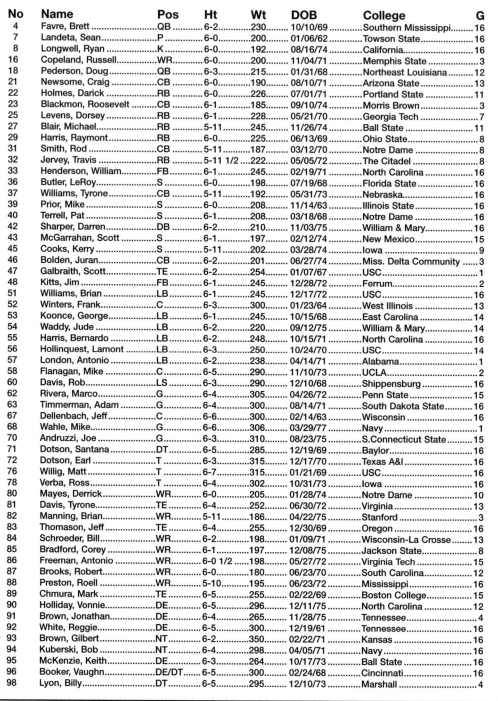

DRAFT

Rnd	Name	Pos	Ht	Wt	College
1a	Vonnie Holliday (19)	DT	6-5	296	North Carolina

(Packers traded 1st-round (29) and 2nd-round (60) picks to Dolphins for Dolphins' 1st-round (19) pick)

Rnd	Name	Pos	Ht	Wt	College
1b	(Choice (29) to Dolphins in deal mentioned above)				
2	(Choice (60) to Dolphins in deal mentioned above)				
3	Jonathan Brown (90)	DE	6-4	268	Tennessee
4	Roosevelt Blackmon (121)	DB	6-1	185	Morris Brown
5a	Corey Bradford (150)	WR	6-1	197	Jackson State

(Choice from Chiefs for Wayne Simmons)

Rnd	Name	Pos	Ht	Wt	College
5b	(Choice (152) to Raiders for Raiders' 6th-round pick (156) and Raiders' 6th-round pick (188) in 1999)				
6a	Scott McGarrahan (156)	S	6-1	200	New Mexico

(Choice from Raiders in deal mentioned above)

Rnd	Name	Pos	Ht	Wt	College
6b	(Choice (182) to Jacksonville for Paul Frase)				
6c	Matt Hasselbeck (187)	QB	6-4	222	Boston College

(Free agency compensatory pick)

Rnd	Name	Pos	Ht	Wt	College
7	Edwin Watson (218)	RB	6-0	224	Purdue

For a player born and raised in steamy Mississippi, Favre seemed to be at his best when the weather turned its worst in Green Bay. Such was the case as he led the Packers past Tennessee 30-22 in 1998 during a December snow fall in Lambeau.

Did You Know?

● Because of injuries, the Packers' running game was a mess. Favre's one TD run left him only one TD behind the team leader in rushing TDs, fullback William Henderson.

1999

Team	Games	Att	Cmp	Yds	Cmp%	Y/Att	TD	Int	Rate
Green Bay	16	595	341	4,091	57.3	6.9	22	23	74.7

Favre Highlights

Led the league and had a career high with 595 passing attempts, finishing with 4,091 yards and a disappointing 22 TDs and 23 interceptions. Played most of the year with a sprained thumb on his throwing hand. Passed Ron Jaworski on the consecutive games list for a QB when he reached 117 straight in the middle of the season. Had a great game in a win at San Francisco with two TDs, a 69 percent completion percentage and 106.4 passer rating.

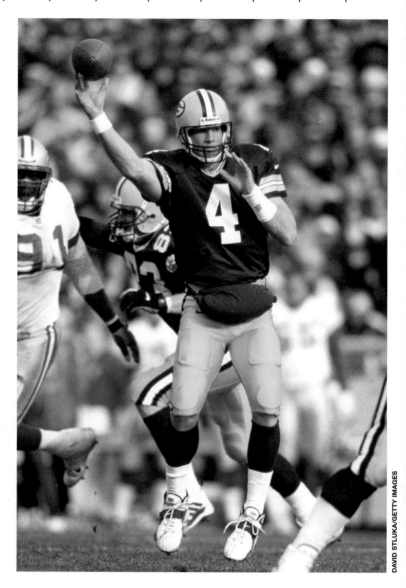

DAVID STLUKA/GETTY IMAGES

DAVID STLUKA/GETTY IMAGES

Team Summary

Record: 8-8

Playoffs: Missed playoffs for the first time since 1992.

Highlights: Ray Rhodes lasted one season as head coach. Dorsey Levens had 1,034 yards rushing and nine TDs. Antonio Freeman and Bill Schroeder each reached 1,000 yards receiving.

Did You Know?

- Favre ran for five first downs in a game against Carolina.

- Favre's 57.3 completion percentage was the lowest of his career.

GAME	DATE	OPPONENT	W/L	GB	Op.	LOCATION
1.	09-12-99	Oakland Raiders	Win	28	24	Home
2.	09-19-99	Detroit Lions	Loss	15	23	Away
3.	09-26-99	Minnesota Vikings	Win	23	20	Home
4.	10-10-99	Tampa Bay Buccaneers	Win	26	23	Home
5.	10-17-99	Denver Broncos	Loss	10	31	Away
6.	10-24-99	San Diego Chargers	Win	31	3	Away
7.	11-01-99	Seattle Seahawks	Loss	7	27	Home
8.	11-07-99	Chicago Bears	Loss	13	14	Home
9.	11-14-99	Dallas Cowboys	Loss	13	27	Away
10.	11-21-99	Detroit Lions	Win	26	17	Home
11.	11-29-99	San Francisco 49ers	Win	20	3	Away
12.	12-05-99	Chicago Bears	Win	35	19	Away
13.	12-12-99	Carolina Panthers	Loss	31	33	Home
14.	12-20-99	Minnesota Vikings	Loss	20	24	Away
15.	12-26-99	Tampa Bay Buccaneers	Loss	10	29	Away
16.	01-02-00	Arizona Cardinals	Win	49	24	Home

Favre scrambles from the clutches of the Vikings' Dwayne Rudd during the Packers 23-20 victory. Packers' coach Ray Rhodes wasn't as fortunate; he was sacked after one season and an 8-8 record.

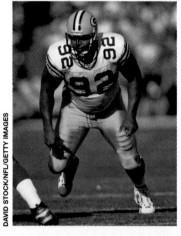

DAVID STOCK/NFL/GETTY IMAGES

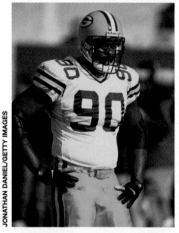

JONATHAN DANIEL/GETTY IMAGES

DAVID STLUKA/GETTY IMAGES

ROSTER

No	Name	Pos	Ht	Wt	DOB	College	G
4	Favre, Brett	QB	6-2	220	10/10/69	Southern Mississippi	16
7	Hanson, Chris	P	6-1	214	10/25/76	Marshall	1
8	Longwell, Ryan	K	6-0	197	08/16/74	California	16
10	Aguiar, Louie	P	6-2	220	06/30/66	Utah State	15
11	Hasselbeck, Matt	QB	6-4	220	09/25/75	Boston College	16
22	Parker, De'Mond	RB	5-10	188	12/24/76	Oklahoma	11
24	Edwards, Antuan	CB	6-1	205	05/26/77	Clemson	16
25	Levens, Dorsey	RB	6-1	228	05/21/70	Georgia Tech	14
27	McBride, Tod	DB	6-1	208	01/26/76	UCLA	15
28	Mitchell, Basil	RB	5-10	200	09/07/75	Texas Christian	16
31	Vinson, Fred	CB	5-11	180	04/02/77	Vanderbilt	16
33	Henderson, William	FB	6-1	250	02/19/71	North Carolina	16
34	McKenzie, Mike	CB	6-0	190	04/26/76	Memphis	16
36	Butler, LeRoy	S	6-0	203	07/19/68	Florida State	16
37	Williams, Tyrone	CB	5-11	195	05/31/73	Nebraska	16
38	Snider, Matt	FB	6-2	243	01/26/76	Richmond	8
42	Sharper, Darren	DB	6-2	210	11/03/75	William & Mary	16
43	McGarrahan, Scott	S	6-1	197	02/12/74	New Mexico	13
45	Crawford, Keith	CB	6-2	198	11/21/70	Howard Payne	3
46	Artmore, Rodney	S	6-0	210	06/14/74	Baylor	5
47	Bell, Tyrone	CB	6-2	210	10/20/74	North Alabama	1
50	Davis, Anthony	LB	6-0	235	03/07/69	Utah	14
51	Williams, Brian	LB	6-1	245	12/17/72	USC	7
52	Winters, Frank	C	6-3	305	01/23/64	West Illinois	16
53	Koonce, George	LB	6-1	245	10/15/68	East Carolina	15
54	Waddy, Jude	LB	6-2	220	09/12/75	William & Mary	16
55	Harris, Bernardo	LB	6-2	250	10/15/71	North Carolina	16
56	Mays, Kivuusama	LB	6-3	248	01/07/75	North Carolina	3
57	Nelson, Jim	LB	6-1	238	04/16/75	Penn State	16
58	Flanagan, Mike	C	6-5	295	11/10/73	UCLA	15
60	Davis, Rob	LS	6-3	285	12/10/68	Shippensburg	16
61	Curry, Scott	T	6-5	300	12/25/75	Montana	5
62	Rivera, Marco	G	6-4	305	04/26/72	Penn State	16
63	McKenzie, Raleigh	G	6-2	290	02/08/63	Tennessee	16
68	Wahle, Mike	G	6-6	306	03/29/77	Navy	16
70	Andruzzi, Joe	G	6-3	310	08/23/75	S. Connecticut State	8
71	Dotson, Santana	DT	6-5	290	12/19/69	Baylor	12
72	Dotson, Earl	T	6-3	310	12/17/70	Texas A&I	15
74	Dingle, Antonio	DT	6-2	315	10/07/76	Virginia	6
75	Heimburger, Craig	G/T	6-2	318	02/03/77	Missouri	2
78	Verba, Ross	T	6-4	308	10/31/73	Iowa	11
80	Driver, Donald	WR	6-0	175	02/02/75	Alcorn State	6
81	Davis, Tyrone	TE	6-4	255	06/30/72	Virginia	16
82	Howard, Desmond	WR	5-10	180	05/15/70	Michigan	8
82	Jordan, Charles	WR	5-10	175	10/09/69	Long Beach City College	4
83	Thomason, Jeff	TE	6-4	255	12/30/69	Oregon	14
84	Schroeder, Bill	WR	6-2	205	01/09/71	Wisconsin-La Crosse	16
85	Bradford, Corey	WR	6-1	205	12/08/75	Jackson State	16
86	Freeman, Antonio	WR	6-0 1/2	198	05/27/72	Virginia Tech	16
88	Arnold, Jahine	WR	6-0	180	06/19/73	Fresno State	1
88	Hall, Lamont	TE	6-4	260	11/16/74	Clemson	14
89	Chmura, Mark	TE	6-5	255	02/22/69	Boston College	2
90	Holliday, Vonnie	DE	6-5	300	12/11/75	North Carolina	16
93	Brown, Gilbert	NT	6-2	345	02/22/71	Kansas	16
94	Barker, Roy	DE	6-5	290	02/24/69	North Carolina	1
95	McKenzie, Keith	DE	6-3	266	10/17/73	Ball State	13
96	Booker, Vaughn	DE/DT	6-5	300	02/24/68	Cincinnati	14
97	Hunt, Cletidus	DE	6-4	295	01/02/76	Kentucky State	11
98	Lyon, Billy	DT	6-5	300	12/10/73	Marshall	16
99	Smith, Jermaine	DT	6-3	298	02/03/72	Georgia	10

DRAFT

Rnd	Name	Pos	Ht	Wt	College
1	Antuan Edwards (25)	DB	6-1	205	Clemson
2a	Fred Vinson (47)	DB	5-11	180	Vanderbilt
	(Choice from Seahawks for Mike Holmgren)				
2b	(Choice exercised for Mike Wahle in 1998 supplemental draft)				
3a	Mike McKenzie (87)	DB	6-0	190	Memphis
3b	Cletidus Hunt (94)	DE	6-4	295	Kentucky State
	(Free agency compensatory pick)				
4a	(Choice (122) to Bills for Darick Holmes)				
4b	Aaron Brooks (131)	QB	6-4	205	Virginia
	(Free agency compensatory pick)				
4c	Josh Bidwell (133)	P	6-3	225	Oregon
	(Free agency compensatory pick)				
5a	De'Mond Parker (159)	RB	5-10	188	Oklahoma

Rnd	Name	Pos	Ht	Wt	College
5b	Craig Heimburger (163)	G	6-2	318	Missouri
	(Choice from Raiders for Packers' 6th round-pick (188))				
6a	(Choice (188) from Raiders in 1998 draft day trade; traded back to Raiders for Raiders' 5th round pick (163) in 1999)				
6b	Dee Miller (196)	WR	5-11	194	Ohio State
6c	Scott Curry (203)	T	6-5	295	Montana
	(Free agency compensatory pick)				
7a	Chris Akins (212)	S	5-11	194	Ark.-Pine Bluff
	(Choice from Rams for Steve Bono)				
7b	Donald Driver (213)	WR	6-0	180	Alcorn State
	(Choice from Bears for Glyn Milburn)				
7c	(Choice (232) to Lions for Glyn Milburn)				

On Nov. 7, 1999, Favre started his 117th consecutive game to break former Philadelphia Eagle Ron Jaworski's record for most consecutive starts by a quarterback.

By The Numbers...

126 Reached 30,000 yards passing in his 126th game, third in league history behind only Dan Marino and Warren Moon.

8 Threw for 3,000 yards for the eighth straight season.

2000

Team	Games	Att	Cmp	Yds	Cmp%	Y/Att	TD	Int	Rate
Green Bay	16	580	338	3,812	58.3	6.6	20	16	78.0

Favre Highlights

Led the NFC with 580 passing attempts and threw for 3,812 yards. Again rushed for more than 100 yards in what would be the final year of nine straight years accomplishing that feat. Exhibited his trademark toughness, returning from an ankle injury against Tampa Bay to throw for 301 yards and two TDS in a 26-24 upset of the Colts the following week.

GEORGE GOJKOVICH /GETTY IMAGES

JONATHAN DANIEL/GETTY IMAGES

Team Summary

Record: 9-7
Playoffs: Missed postseason
Highlights: Ahman Green emerged as the team's leading rusher (1,175 yards) and receiver (73 catches). Bill Schroeder fell a yard short of 1,000 yards receiving, while Antonio Freeman had nine TDs.

GAME	DATE	OPPONENT	W/L	GB	Op.	LOCATION
1.	09-03-00	New York Jets	Loss	16	20	Home
2.	09-10-00	Buffalo Bills	Loss	18	27	Away
3.	09-17-00	Philadelphia Eagles	Win	6	3	Home
4.	09-24-00	Arizona Cardinals	Win	29	3	Away
5.	10-01-00	Chicago Bears	Loss	24	27	Home
6.	10-08-00	Detroit Lions	Loss	24	31	Away
7.	10-15-00	San Francisco 49ers	Win	31	28	Home
8.	10-29-00	Miami Dolphins	Loss	20	28	Away
9.	11-06-00	Minnesota Vikings	Win	26	20	Home
10.	11-12-00	Tampa Bay Buccaneers	Loss	15	20	Away
11.	11-19-00	Indianapolis Colts	Win	26	24	Home
12.	11-27-00	Carolina Panthers	Loss	14	31	Away
13.	12-03-00	Chicago Bears	Win	28	6	Away
14.	12-10-00	Detroit Lions	Win	26	13	Home
15.	12-17-00	Minnesota Vikings	Win	33	28	Away
16.	12-24-00	Tampa Bay Buccaneers	Win	17	14	Home

Favre faced Peyton Manning of the Colts for the first time on November 19, 2000, with the Packers winning 26-24 in Lambeau.

By The Numbers...

141 Favre reached 250 TD passes in 141 games, second-fastest in history behind Dan Marino.

20 Favre's four late comebacks in Lambeau Field in the 2000 season raised his career total to 20.

ROSTER

TOM HAUCK/GETTY IMAGES

JONATHAN DANIEL/GETTY IMAGES

DAVID STLUKA/GETTY IMAGES

No	Name	Pos	Ht	Wt	DOB	College	G
4	Favre, Brett	QB	6-2	225	10/10/69	Southern Mississippi	16
7	Wuerffel, Danny	QB	6-1	212	05/27/74	Florida	1
8	Longwell, Ryan	K	6-0	198	08/16/74	California	16
9	Bidwell, Josh	P	6-3	222	03/13/76	Oregon	16
11	Hasselbeck, Matt	QB	6-4	220	09/25/75	Boston College	16
20	Rossum, Allen	CB/KR	5-8	178	10/22/75	Notre Dame	16
21	Berry, Gary	S	5-11	193	10/24/77	Ohio State	4
22	Parker, De'Mond	RB	5-10	185	12/24/76	Oklahoma	8
24	Edwards, Antuan	CB	6-1	205	05/26/77	Clemson	12
25	Levens, Dorsey	RB	6-1	230	05/21/70	Georgia Tech	5
27	McBride, Tod	DB	6-1	207	01/26/76	UCLA	15
28	Mitchell, Basil	RB	5-10	200	09/07/75	Texas Christian	1
29	Goodman, Herbert	RB	5-11	203	08/31/77	Graceland	5
30	Green, Ahman	RB	6-0	217	02/16/77	Nebraska	16
31	Akins, Chris	S	5-11	195	11/29/76	Arkansas-Pine Bluff	2
33	Henderson, William	FB	6-1	253	02/19/71	North Carolina	16
34	McKenzie, Mike	CB	6-0	185	04/26/76	Memphis	10
36	Butler, LeRoy	S	6-0	203	07/19/68	Florida State	16
37	Williams, Tyrone	CB	5-11	193	05/31/73	Nebraska	16
40	Moore, Jason	S	5-10	191	01/15/76	San Diego State	3
42	Sharper, Darren	DB	6-2	205	11/03/75	William & Mary	16
43	McGarrahan, Scott	S	6-1	198	02/12/74	New Mexico	16
44	Snider, Matt	FB	6-2	240	01/26/76	Richmond	16
50	Williams, K.D.	LB	6-0	235	04/22/73	Henderson State	16
51	Williams, Brian	LB	6-1	245	12/17/72	USC	4
52	Winters, Frank	C	6-3	305	01/23/64	West Illinois	14
53	Morton, Mike	LB	6-4	238	03/28/72	North Carolina	16
54	Wayne, Nate	LB	6-0	230	01/12/75	Mississippi	16
55	Harris, Bernardo	LB	6-2	246	10/15/71	North Carolina	16
56	McCaslin, Eugene	LB	6-1	226	07/12/77	Florida	1
57	Gizzi, Chris	LB	6-0	235	03/08/75	Air Force	11
58	Flanagan, Mike	C	6-5	297	11/10/73	UCLA	16
59	Diggs, Na'il	LB	6-4	234	07/08/78	Ohio State	13
60	Davis, Rob	LS	6-3	285	12/10/68	Shippensburg	16
62	Rivera, Marco	G	6-4	310	04/26/72	Penn State	16
63	McKenzie, Raleigh	G	6-2	290	02/08/63	Tennessee	3
65	Tauscher, Mark	T	6-3	313	06/17/77	Wisconsin	16
67	Maryland, Russell	DT	6-1	308	03/22/69	Miami (FL)	16
68	Wahle, Mike	G	6-6	310	03/29/77	Navy	16
71	Dotson, Santana	DT	6-5	290	12/19/69	Baylor	12
72	Dotson, Earl	T	6-3	317	12/17/70	Texas A&I	2
76	Clifton, Chad	T	6-5	325	06/26/76	Tennessee	13
78	Verba, Ross	T	6-4	308	10/31/73	Iowa	16
79	Stokes, Barry	G/T	6-4	310	12/20/73	Eastern Michigan	8
80	Driver, Donald	WR	6-0	177	02/02/75	Alcorn State	16
81	Davis, Tyrone	TE	6-4	260	06/30/72	Virginia	14
82	Lee, Charles	WR	6-2	202	11/19/77	Central Florida	15
83	Wetnight, Ryan	TE	6-2	230	11/05/70	Stanford	10
84	Schroeder, Bill	WR	6-2	205	01/09/71	Wisconsin-La Crosse	16
85	Bradford, Corey	WR	6-1	205	12/08/75	Jackson State	2
86	Freeman, Antonio	WR	6-0 1/2	198	05/27/72	Virginia Tech	15
88	Franks, Bubba	TE	6-6	260	01/06/78	Miami (FL)	16
90	Holliday, Vonnie	DE	6-5	290	12/11/75	North Carolina	12
91	Thierry, John	DE	6-4	262	09/04/71	Alcorn State	16
94	Gbaja-Biamila, Kabeer	DE	6-4	245	09/24/77	San Diego State	7
95	Warren, Steve	DT	6-1	298	01/22/78	Nebraska	13
96	Bowens, David	DE	6-2	261	07/03/77	Western Illinois	14
97	Hunt, Cletidus	DE	6-4	299	01/02/76	Kentucky State	16
98	Lyon, Billy	DE/DT	6-5	295	12/10/73	Marshall	11
99	Robbins, Austin	DT	6-6	300	03/01/71	North Carolina	2

DRAFT

Rnd	Name	Pos	Ht	Wt	College
1	Bubba Franks (14)	TE	6-6	260	Miami (FL)
2	Chad Clifton (44)	T	6-5	325	Tennessee
3	Steve Warren (74)	DT	6-1	298	Nebraska
4a	Na'il Diggs (98)	LB	6-4	234	Ohio State
	(Choice from 49ers for Packers' 4th-round (108) and 5th-round (132) picks)				
4b	(Choice (108) from Jets for Rick Mirer; to 49ers in deal mentioned above)				
4c	Anthony Lucas (114)	WR	6-2	197	Arkansas
4d	Gary Berry (126)	S	5-11	193	Ohio State
	(Free agent compensatory pick)				
5a	(Choice (132) from 49ers for Craig Newsome; to 49ers in deal mentioned above)				
5b	Kabeer Gbaja-Biamila (149)	DE	6-4	245	San Diego State

Rnd	Name	Pos	Ht	Wt	College
5c	Joey Jamison (151)	WR	5-9	167	Texas Southern
	(from Seahawks in Ahman Green/Fred Vinson trade)				
6	(Choice (185) to Seahawks in Ahman Green/Fred Vinson trade)				
7a	Mark Tauscher (224)	T	6-3	313	Wisconsin
7b	Ron Moore (229)	DT	6-4	295	NW Oklahoma
	(Choice from Seahawks for Derrick Mayes)				
7c	Charles Lee (242)	WR	6-2	200	Central Florida
	(Free agent compensatory pick)				
7d	Eugene McCaslin (249)	LB	6-1	225	Florida
	(Free agent compensatory pick)				
7e	Rondell Mealey (252)	RB	5-11	209	LSU
	(Free agency compensatory pick)				

Did You Know?

● The Packers won their final four games and five of their last six in 2000, propelling them into a 2001 season that would end their two-year playoff drought.

Favre's favorite receiver in 2000 proved to be the team's leading rusher. Ahman Green caught 73 passes and ran for 1,175 yards and 10 touchdowns.

2001

Team	Games	Att	Cmp	Yds	Cmp%	Y/Att	TD	Int	Rate
Green Bay	16	510	314	3,921	61.6	7.7	32	15	94.1

Favre Highlights

Finished second in the NFC with 3,921 yards passing and second in the NFL with 32 TD passes with only 15 interceptions. Earned the sixth Pro Bowl berth of his career and fourth as a starter. Was also the leading vote-getter. Had an amazing day Dec. 3 vs. Jacksonville: 362 yards and three TDs with no interceptions, plus the winning score on a 6-yard bootleg with 1:30 remaining. Threw six interceptions, tied for the most ever, in the ugly 45-17 thumping at St. Louis in the playoffs.

Went 8-5 record as a starter and broke two Green Bay passing records – single-season marks for passing percentage (64.12 percent) and most consecutive 200-yard passing games (11).

JEFF KOWALSKY/AFP/GETTY IMAGES

JAMES BIEVER/NFL PHOTOS/GETTY IMAGES

Team Summary

Record: 12-4, Wild Card
Playoffs: Beat the 49ers at home but lost at St. Louis in one of the worst blowouts in team history.
Highlights: Ahman Green had 1,387 yards rushing and nine TDs and again led the team in receptions (62). Favre spread the ball to seven receivers with 20+ catches each.

JAMES BIEVER/NFL PHOTOS/GETTY

GAME	DATE	OPPONENT	W/L	GB	Op.	LOCATION
1.	09-09-2001	Detroit Lions	Win	28	6	Home
2.	09-24-2001	Washington Redskins	Win	37	0	Home
3.	09-30-2001	Carolina Panthers	Win	28	7	Away
4.	10-07-2001	Tampa Bay Buccaneers	Loss	10	14	Away
5.	10-14-2001	Baltimore Ravens	Win	31	23	Home
6.	10-21-2001	Minnesota Vikings	Loss	13	35	Away
7.	11-04-2001	Tampa Bay Buccaneers	Win	21	20	Home
8.	11-11-2001	Chicago Bears	Win	20	12	Away
9.	11-18-2001	Atlanta Falcons	Loss	20	23	Home
10.	11-22-2001	Detroit Lions	Win	29	27	Away
11.	12-03-2001	Jacksonville Jaguars	Win	28	21	Away
12.	12-09-2001	Chicago Bears	Win	17	7	Home
13.	12-16-2001	Tennessee Titans	Loss	20	26	Away
14.	12-23-2001	Cleveland Browns	Win	30	7	Home
15.	12-30-2001	Minnesota Vikings	Win	24	13	Home
16.	01-06-2002	New York Giants	Win	34	25	Away
17.	01-13-2002	San Francisco 49ers	Win	25	15	Home
18.	01-20-2002	St. Louis Rams	Loss	17	45	Away

One of the Packers best games of 2001 saw them beat the defending Super Bowl champion Baltimore Ravens 31-23 at Lambeau. Favre passed for 337 yards and three touchdowns.

By The Numbers...

30 Favre reached 300 yards in a game for the 30th time, topping the mark against the champion Ravens' vaunted defense.

53 Number of games between rushing TDs for Favre when he finally ran one in on Dec. 3.

22 Favre recorded his 22nd comeback victory in his career, a home win against the Vikings.

ROSTER

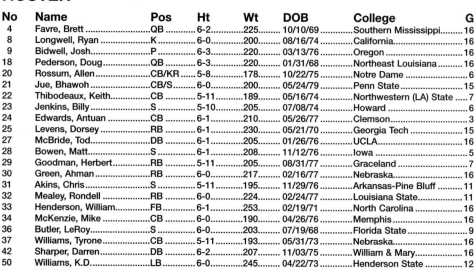

No	Name	Pos	Ht	Wt	DOB	College	G
4	Favre, Brett	QB	6-2	225	10/10/69	Southern Mississippi	16
8	Longwell, Ryan	K	6-0	200	08/16/74	California	16
9	Bidwell, Josh	P	6-3	220	03/13/76	Oregon	16
18	Pederson, Doug	QB	6-3	220	01/31/68	Northeast Louisiana	16
20	Rossum, Allen	CB/KR	5-8	178	10/22/75	Notre Dame	6
21	Jue, Bhawoh	CB/S	6-0	200	05/24/79	Penn State	15
22	Thibodeaux, Keith	CB	5-11	189	05/16/74	Northwestern (LA) State	7
23	Jenkins, Billy	S	5-10	205	07/08/74	Howard	6
24	Edwards, Antuan	CB	6-1	210	05/26/77	Clemson	3
25	Levens, Dorsey	RB	6-1	230	05/21/70	Georgia Tech	15
27	McBride, Tod	DB	6-1	205	01/26/76	UCLA	16
28	Bowen, Matt	S	6-1	208	11/12/76	Iowa	5
29	Goodman, Herbert	RB	5-11	205	08/31/77	Graceland	7
30	Green, Ahman	RB	6-0	217	02/16/77	Nebraska	16
31	Akins, Chris	S	5-11	195	11/29/76	Arkansas-Pine Bluff	11
32	Mealey, Rondell	RB	6-0	224	02/24/77	Louisiana State	11
33	Henderson, William	FB	6-1	253	02/19/71	North Carolina	16
34	McKenzie, Mike	CB	6-0	190	04/26/76	Memphis	16
36	Butler, LeRoy	S	6-0	203	07/19/68	Florida State	9
37	Williams, Tyrone	CB	5-11	193	05/31/73	Nebraska	16
42	Sharper, Darren	DB	6-2	207	11/03/75	William & Mary	16
50	Williams, K.D.	LB	6-0	245	04/22/73	Henderson State	12
51	Marshall, Torrance	LB	6-2	255	06/12/77	Oklahoma	14
52	Winters, Frank	C	6-3	305	01/23/64	West Illinois	4
53	O'Neal, Andre	LB	6-1	235	12/12/75	Marshall	2
54	Wayne, Nate	LB	6-0	237	01/12/75	Mississippi	12
55	Harris, Bernardo	LB	6-2	250	10/15/71	North Carolina	16
56	Holmberg, Rob	LB	6-3	240	05/06/71	Penn State	4
57	Gizzi, Chris	LB	6-0	235	03/08/75	Air Force	12
58	Flanagan, Mike	C	6-5	297	11/10/73	UCLA	16
59	Diggs, Na'il	LB	6-4	238	07/08/78	Ohio State	16
60	Davis, Rob	LS	6-3	285	12/10/68	Shippensburg	16
62	Rivera, Marco	G	6-4	310	04/26/72	Penn State	16
65	Tauscher, Mark	T	6-3	320	06/17/77	Wisconsin	16
68	Wahle, Mike	G	6-6	310	03/29/77	Navy	16
71	Dotson, Santana	DT	6-5	287	12/19/69	Baylor	16
72	Dotson, Earl	T	6-3	317	12/17/70	Texas A&I	12
75	Flanigan, Jim	DT	6-2	290	08/27/71	Notre Dame	16
76	Clifton, Chad	T	6-5	327	06/26/76	Tennessee	14
79	Stokes, Barry	G/T	6-4	310	12/20/73	Eastern Michigan	16
80	Driver, Donald	WR	6-0	185	02/02/75	Alcorn State	13
81	Davis, Tyrone	TE	6-4	260	06/30/72	Virginia	4
82	Lee, Charles	WR	6-2	205	11/19/77	Central Florida	7
83	Martin, David	TE	6-4	250	03/13/79	Tennessee	14
84	Schroeder, Bill	WR	6-2	205	01/09/71	Wisconsin-La Crosse	14
85	Bradford, Corey	WR	6-1	197	12/08/75	Jackson State	16
86	Freeman, Antonio	WR	6-0 1/2	198	05/27/72	Virginia Tech	16
87	Collins, Bobby	TE	6-4	248	08/26/76	North Alabama	4
88	Franks, Bubba	TE	6-6	260	01/06/78	Miami (FL)	16
89	Ferguson, Robert	WR	6-1	209	12/17/79	Texas A&M	1
90	Holliday, Vonnie	DE	6-5	290	12/11/75	North Carolina	16
91	Thierry, John	DE	6-4	262	09/04/71	Alcorn State	12
93	Brown, Gilbert	DT	6-2	339	02/27/71	Kansas	11
94	Gbaja-Biamila, Kabeer	DE	6-4	253	09/24/77	San Diego State	16
95	Walker, Rod	DT	6-3	320	02/04/76	Troy State	11
97	Hunt, Cletidus	DE/DT	6-4	290	01/02/76	Kentucky State	12
98	Lyon, Billy	DE/DT	6-5	295	12/10/73	Marshall	12
99	Reynolds, Jamal	DE	6-3	266	02/20/79	Florida State	6

Photo credits (vertical): JAMES V. BIEVER/NFL/GETTY IMAGES · JEFF GROSS/GETTY IMAGES · MATT STROSHANE/GETTY IMAGES

DRAFT

Rnd	Name	Pos	Ht	Wt	College
1a	Jamal Reynolds (10)	DE	6-3	266	Florida State
	(Choice from Seahawks in Matt Hasselbeck trade)				
1b	(Choice (17) to Seahawks in Matt Hasselbeck trade)				
2a	Robert Ferguson (41)	WR	6-1	209	Texas A&M
	(Traded 2nd-round (47), two 3rd-round (80 & 82), 6th-round (179) and 7th-rd (222) picks to 49ers for 49ers' 2nd-rd (41), 3rd-rd (71) and 4th-round (105) picks)				
2b	(Choice (47) to 49ers in deal mentioned above)				
3a	Bhawoh Jue (71)	DB	6-0	200	Penn State
	(Choice from 49ers in deal mentioned above)				
3b	Torrance Marshall (72)	LB	6-2	250	Oklahoma
	(Choice from Seahawks in Matt Hasselbeck trade)				
3c	(Choice (80) to 49ers in deal mentioned above)				

Rnd	Name	Pos	Ht	Wt	College
3d	(Choice (82) from Saints in Aaron Brooks/Lamont Hall/K.D. Williams trade; to 49ers in deal mentioned above)				
4a	Bill Ferrario (105)	G	6-2	315	Wisconsin
	(Choice from 49ers in deal mentioned above)				
4b	(Choice (113) to Broncos for Nate Wayne)				
5	(Choice (147) to Eagles for Allen Rossum)				
6a	(Choice (179) to 49ers in deal mentioned above)				
6b	David Martin (198)	TE	6-4	250	Tennessee
	(Free agent compensatory pick)				
7a	(Choice (219) to Broncos for David Bowens)				
7b	(Choice (222) from Rams in Mike Morton trade; to 49ers in deal mentioned above)				

Did You Know?

● Packers fans remember the St. Louis playoff debacle, but in the previous game, against the 49ers, Favre threw for 226 yards in the second half alone, and completed 76 percent of his passes in the game. And in the final seven games of the regular season, he had only two INTs.

2002

Team	Games	Att	Cmp	Yds	Cmp%	Y/Att	TD	Int	Rate
Green Bay	16	551	341	3,658	61.9	6.6	27	16	85.6

Favre Highlights

Led the Packers to their fourth division title and eight playoff berth in his 11 seasons as the starter. Was honored by Sports Illustrated and the *Dallas Morning News* as the NFL Player of the Year, among other honors. Made the Pro Bowl for the seventh time, although he backed out because of injuries, and for the second year in a row was the top vote-getter. Overcame a knee injury that looked very serious against Washington on Oct. 20, but had a bye week to get ready and returned in the next game, a Monday night win against Miami.

JOHN G. MABANGLO/AFP/GETTY IMAGES

DAVID STLUKA/GETTY IMAGES

Team Summary

Record: 12-4, Division Title
Playoffs: Upset at home by Michael Vick and Atlanta in a game in which the Packers were ravaged by injuries and lost at home in the playoffs for the first time ever.
Highlights: Ahman Green had 1,240 yards rushing and Donald Driver had 1,064 yards receiving and nine TDs. The Packers won the NFC Central Division by six games.

GAME	DATE	OPPONENT	W/L	GB	Op.	LOCATION
1.	09-08-02	Atlanta Falcons	Win	37	34	Home
2.	09-15-02	New Orleans Saints	Loss	20	35	Away
3.	09-22-02	Detroit Lions	Win	37	31	Away
4.	09-29-02	Carolina Panthers	Win	17	14	Home
5.	10-07-02	Chicago Bears	Win	34	21	Away
6.	10-13-02	New England Patriots	Win	28	10	Away
7.	10-20-02	Washington Redskins	Win	30	9	Home
8.	11-04-02	Miami Dolphins	Win	24	10	Home
9.	11-10-02	Detroit Lions	Win	40	14	Home
10.	11-17-02	Minnesota Vikings	Loss	21	31	Away
11.	11-24-02	Tampa Bay Buccaneers	Loss	7	21	Away
12.	12-01-02	Chicago Bears	Win	30	20	Home
13.	12-08-02	Minnesota Vikings	Win	26	22	Home
14.	12-15-02	San Francisco 49ers	Win	20	14	Away
15.	12-22-02	Buffalo Bills	Win	10	0	Home
16.	12-29-02	New York Jets	Loss	17	42	Away
17.	01-04-03	Atlanta Falcons	Loss	7	27	Home

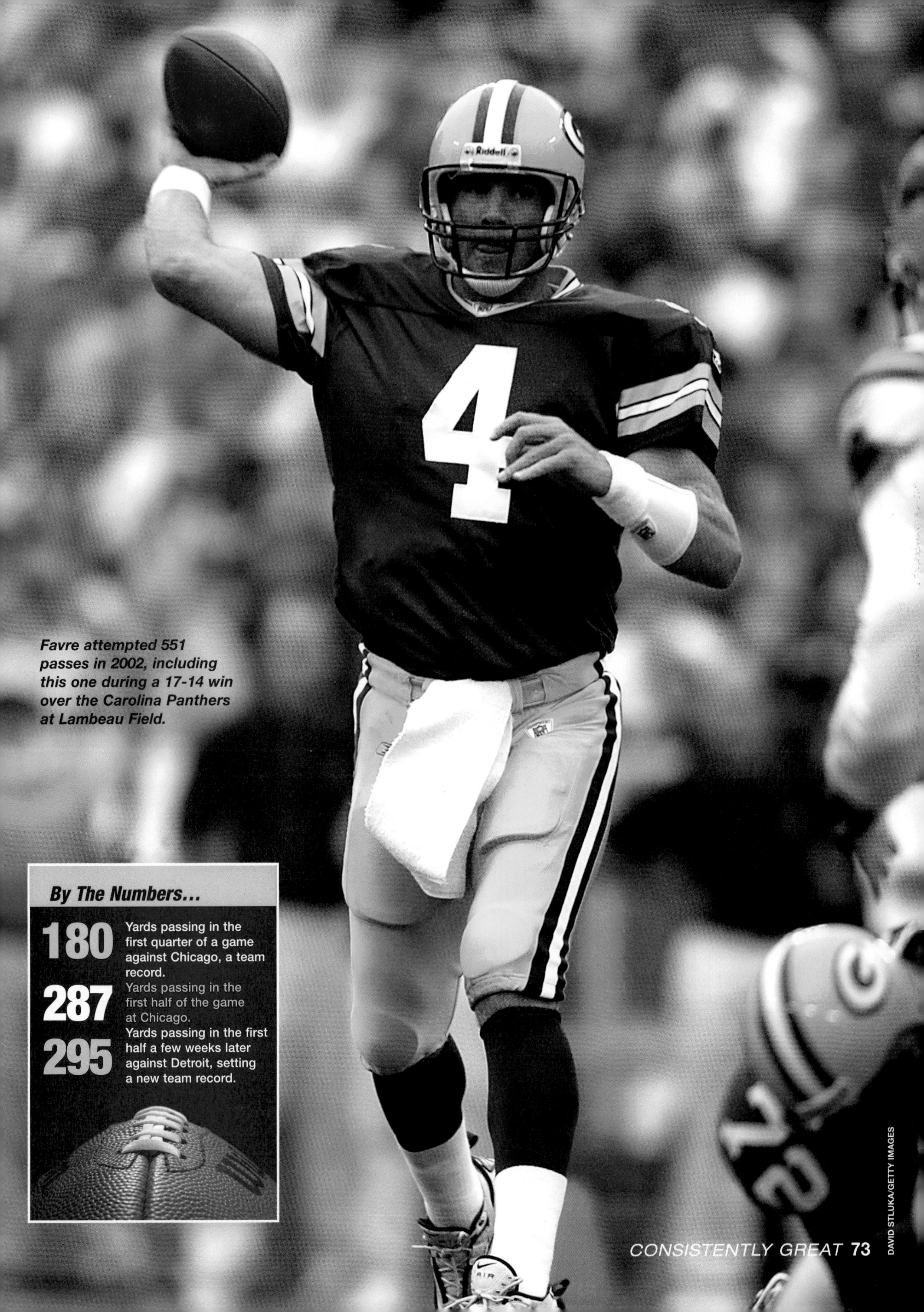

Favre attempted 551 passes in 2002, including this one during a 17-14 win over the Carolina Panthers at Lambeau Field.

By The Numbers...

180 Yards passing in the first quarter of a game against Chicago, a team record.

287 Yards passing in the first half of the game at Chicago.

295 Yards passing in the first half a few weeks later against Detroit, setting a new team record.

DAVID STLUKA/GETTY IMAGES

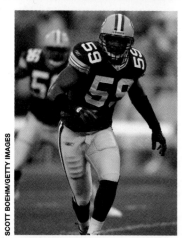

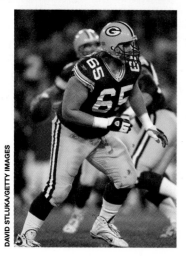

ROSTER

No	Name	Pos	Ht	Wt	DOB	College	G
4	Favre, Brett	QB	6-2	225	10/10/69	Southern Mississippi	16
8	Longwell, Ryan	K	6-0	200	08/16/74	California	16
9	Bidwell, Josh	P	6-3	220	03/13/76	Oregon	16
18	Pederson, Doug	QB	6-3	220	01/31/68	Northeast Louisiana	16
20	Anderson, Marques	S	5-11	212	05/26/79	UCLA	14
21	Jue, Bhawoh	CB/S	6-0	200	05/24/79	Penn State	4
22	Metcalf, Eric	WR	5-10	195	01/23/68	Texas	1
23	Gordon, Darrien	CB/KR	5-11	190	11/14/70	Stanford	13
24	Edwards, Antuan	CB	6-1	210	05/26/77	Clemson	12
26	Swiney, Erwin	DB	6-0	192	10/08/78	Nebraska	3
27	McBride, Tod	DB	6-1	205	01/26/76	UCLA	15
28	Bowen, Matt	S	6-1	210	11/12/76	Iowa	16
30	Green, Ahman	RB	6-0	217	02/16/77	Nebraska	14
32	Mealey, Rondell	RB	6-0	224	02/24/77	Louisiana State	3
32	Westbrook, Bryant	CB	6-1	198	12/19/74	Texas	6
33	Henderson, William	FB	6-1	253	02/19/71	North Carolina	15
34	McKenzie, Mike	CB	6-0	190	04/26/76	Memphis	13
35	Graham, Jay	RB	6-0	225	07/14/76	Tennessee	3
37	Williams, Tyrone	CB	5-11	193	05/31/73	Nebraska	15
39	Carter, Tony	RB	6-0	235	08/23/72	Minnesota	12
40	Fisher, Tony	RB	6-1	222	10/12/79	Notre Dame	15
41/51	Marshall, Torrance	LB	6-2	255	06/12/77	Oklahoma	16
42	Sharper, Darren	DB	6-2	207	11/03/75	William & Mary	13
43	Smith, Maurice (Mo)	RB	6-0	235	02/14/77	North Carolina A&T	1
44	Davenport, Najeh	FB	6-1	247	02/08/79	Miami	8
49	Franz, Todd	CB	6-0	194	04/12/76	Tulsa	2
52	Winters, Frank	C	6-3	305	01/23/64	West Illinois	16
53	Lenon, Paris	LB	6-2	232	11/26/77	Richmond	16
54	Wayne, Nate	LB	6-0	237	01/12/75	Mississippi	16
55	Wilkins, Marcus	LB	6-2	231	01/02/80	Texas	5
56	Nickerson, Hardy	LB	6-2	237	09/01/65	California	16
58	Flanagan, Mike	C	6-5	297	11/10/73	UCLA	16
59	Diggs, Na'il	LB	6-4	238	07/08/78	Ohio State	16
60	Davis, Rob	LS	6-3	285	12/10/68	Shippensburg	16
62	Rivera, Marco	G	6-4	310	04/26/72	Penn State	16
63	Ferrario, Bill	G	6-2	315	09/22/78	Wisconsin	16
64	Jackson, Alcender	G/T	6-3	311	05/18/77	Louisiana State	2
65	Tauscher, Mark	T	6-3	320	06/17/77	Wisconsin	2
68	Wahle, Mike	G	6-6	310	03/29/77	Navy	16
69	Blackshear, Jeff	G	6-6	323	03/29/69	Northeast Louisiana	1
71	Barry, Kevin	T	6-4	325	07/20/79	Arizona	14
72	Dotson, Earl	T	6-3	317	12/17/70	Texas A&I	14
73	McKenzie, Keith	DE	6-3	270	10/17/73	Ball State	4
74	Kampman, Aaron	DE	6-4	287	11/30/79	Iowa	12
75	Tomich, Jared	DE	6-3	283	04/24/74	Nebraska	2
76	Clifton, Chad	T	6-5	327	06/26/76	Tennessee	10
77	Brooks, Barrett	T	6-4	320	05/05/72	Kansas State	2
77	Wisne, Jerry	T	6-6	315	07/28/76	Notre Dame	2
80	Driver, Donald	WR	6-0	185	02/02/75	Alcorn State	16
81	Davis, Tyrone	TE	6-4	260	06/30/72	Virginia	9
83	Glenn, Terry	WR	5-11	195	07/23/74	Ohio State	15
84	Walker, Javon	WR	6-3	210	10/14/78	Florida State	15
85	Bailey, Karsten	WR	6-0	205	04/26/77	Auburn	7
86	Jackson, Chris	WR	6-2	204	02/26/75	Washington State	1
86	Moses, J.J.	WR/KR	5-6	178	09/12/79	Iowa State	2
87	Martin, David	TE	6-4	250	03/13/79	Tennessee	8
88	Franks, Bubba	TE	6-6	260	01/06/78	Miami (FL)	16
89	Ferguson, Robert	WR	6-1	209	12/17/79	Texas A&M	16
90	Holliday, Vonnie	DE	6-5	290	12/11/75	North Carolina	10
91	Johnson, Joe	DE	6-4	275	07/11/72	Louisville	5
93	Brown, Gilbert	DT	6-2	339	02/22/71	Kansas	12
94	Gbaja-Biamila, Kabeer	DE	6-4	253	09/24/77	San Diego State	15
95	Walker, Rod	DT	6-3	320	02/04/76	Troy State	13
96	Warren, Steve	DT	6-1	298	01/22/78	Nebraska	12
97	Hunt, Cletidus	DE/DT	6-4	299	01/02/76	Kentucky State	14
98	Lyon, Billy	DE/DT	6-5	295	12/10/73	Marshall	16
99	Reynolds, Jamal	DE	6-3	266	02/20/79	Florida State	7

DRAFT

Rnd	Name	Pos	Ht	Wt	College
1a	Javon Walker (20)	WR	6-3	215	Florida State

(Traded 1st-round (28) and 2nd-round (60) picks to Seahawks for Seahawks' 1st-round (20) and 5th-round (156) picks)

1b	(Choice (28) to Seahawks in deal mentioned above)				
2	(Choice (60) to Seahawks in deal mentioned above)				
3	Marques Anderson (92)	S	5-11	213	UCLA
4a	(Choice (126) to Patriots for Terry Glenn)				
4b	Najeh Davenport (135)	RB	6-1	248	Miami

(Free agency compensatory pick)

Rnd	Name	Pos	Ht	Wt	College
5a	Aaron Kampman (156)	DE	6-4	285	Iowa

(Choice from Seahawks in deal mentioned above)

5b	Craig Nall (164)	QB	6-3	237	Northwestern State
6	Mike Houghton (200)	G	6-5	318	San Diego State
7	(Choice (240) to Titans for Rod Walker)				

Referee Dick Hantak, who retired after the 2002 season, and Favre share a hug near the end of the fourth quarter of the Jets' 42-17 win over the Packers at Giants Stadium.

Did You Know?

● Brett Favre passed John Unitas (290), Warren Moon (291) and John Elway (300) in becoming the eighth 300-TD passer in NFL history.

● In the playoff loss to Atlanta, Favre tied Dan Marino's mark with a TD pass in 13 straight postseason games.

CONSISTENTLY GREAT **75**

2003

Team	Games	Att	Cmp	Yds	Cmp%	Y/Att	TD	Int	Rate
Green Bay	16	471	308	3,361	65.4	7.1	32	21	90.4

Favre Highlights

Possibly Favre's most amazing year in which he played with a fractured thumb and through the death of his father. Green Bay won its fifth division title and made its ninth playoff appearance in Favre's 12 years as a starter. Led the NFL with 32 TD passes. His best performance ever could have been the 41-7 win over Oakland on Monday night, Dec. 22, the day after his father Irv died. He had four TD passes and a team-record 154.9 passer rating while also passing Fran Tarkenton for second on the all-time TD throwing list with 343. He also threw four TD passes the week before against San Diego.

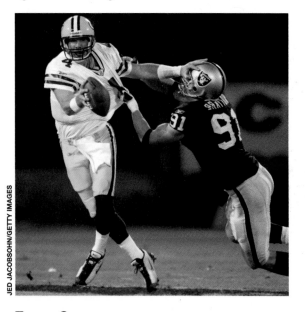

Team Summary

Record: 10-6, Division Title
Playoffs: Beat Seattle in the first round on Al Harris' interception return in overtime, then lost the heartbreaker in overtime at Philadelphia in which the Eagles converted on fourth-and-26 on the way to the tying field goal in regulation.
Highlights: Ahman Green set a team record with 1,883 yards rushing with 15 TDs, and Javon Walker had a breakout year with nine TD catches.

GAME	DATE	OPPONENT	W/L	GB	Op.	LOCATION
1.	09-07-03	Minnesota Vikings	Loss	25	30	Home
2.	09-14-03	Detroit Lions	Win	31	6	Home
3.	09-21-03	Arizona Cardinals	Loss	13	20	Away
4.	09-29-03	Chicago Bears	Win	38	23	Away
5.	10-05-03	Seattle Seahawks	Win	35	13	Home
6.	10-12-03	Kansas City Chiefs	Loss	34	40	Home
7.	10-19-03	St. Louis Rams	Loss	24	34	Away
8.	11-02-03	Minnesota Vikings	Win	30	27	Away
9.	11-10-03	Philadelphia Eagles	Loss	14	17	Home
10.	11-16-03	Tampa Bay Buccaneers	Win	20	13	Away
11.	11-23-03	San Francisco 49ers	Win	20	10	Home
12.	11-27-03	Detroit Lions	Loss	14	22	Away
13.	12-07-03	Chicago Bears	Win	34	21	Home
14.	12-14-03	San Diego Chargers	Win	38	21	Away
15.	12-22-03	Oakland Raiders	Win	41	7	Away
16.	12-28-03	Denver Broncos	Win	31	3	Home
17.	01-04-04	Seattle Seahawks	Win	33	27	Home
18.	01-11-04	Philadelphia Eagles	Loss	17	20	Away

Always one to show his emotions, Favre leaps in celebration with teammate Javon Walker after a touchdown during the Packers 31-3 throttling of the Denver Broncos.

By The Numbers...

30 Favre reached 30 career comeback wins with a victory against the Seahawks in the play-offs.

23 Favre's streak of 23 consecutive games with a TD pass surpassed Cecil Isbell for the team record and would later reach the 30s.

15 Favre set a new NFL record for consecutive playoff games with a TD pass.

2003

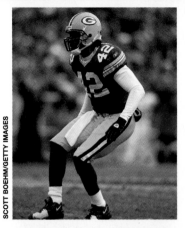

ROSTER

No	Name	Pos	Ht	Wt	DOB	College	G
4	Favre, Brett	QB	6-2	225	10/10/69	Southern Mississippi	16
8	Longwell, Ryan	K	6-0	200	08/16/74	California	16
9	Bidwell, Josh	P	6-3	220	03/13/76	Oregon	16
16	Nall, Craig	QB	6-3	230	04/21/79	Northwestern (LA) State	1
18	Pederson, Doug	QB	6-3	220	01/31/68	Northeast Louisiana	16
20	Anderson, Marques	S	5-11	212	05/26/79	UCLA	16
21	Jue, Bhawoh	CB/S	6-0	200	05/24/79	Penn State	16
22	Luchey, Nick	FB	6-2	270	03/30/77	Miami (FL)	10
24	Edwards, Antuan	CB	6-1	212	05/26/77	Clemson	10
25	Whitley, James	DB	5-11	190	05/13/79	Michigan	3
26	Swiney, Erwin	DB	6-0	192	10/08/78	Nebraska	6
27	Hawthorne, Michael	S/CB	6-3	200	01/26/77	Purdue	14
29	Fuller, Curtis	S	5-11	191	07/25/78	Texas Christian	9
30	Green, Ahman	RB	6-0	217	02/16/77	Nebraska	16
31	Harris, Al	CB	6-1	185	12/07/74	Texas A&M-Kingsville	16
33	Henderson, William	FB	6-1	253	02/19/71	North Carolina	16
34	McKenzie, Mike	CB	6-0	194	04/26/76	Memphis	14
40	Fisher, Tony	RB	6-1	222	10/12/79	Notre Dame	15
42	Sharper, Darren	DB	6-2	207	11/03/75	William & Mary	15
44	Davenport, Najeh	FB	6-1	245	02/08/79	Miami (FL)	15
45	Combs, Derek	CB	6-0	185	02/28/79	Ohio State	8
50	Navies, Hannibal	LB	6-3	247	07/19/77	Colorado	16
51	Marshall, Torrance	LB	6-2	255	06/12/77	Oklahoma	12
53	Lenon, Paris	LB	6-2	240	11/26/77	Richmond	16
55	Wilkins, Marcus	LB	6-2	235	01/02/80	Texas	8
56	Barnett, Nick	LB	6-2	240	05/27/81	Oregon State	15
57	Slaughter, T.J.	LB	6-0	233	02/20/77	Southern Mississippi	1
58	Flanagan, Mike	C	6-5	297	11/10/73	UCLA	16
59	Diggs, Na'il	LB	6-4	238	07/08/78	Ohio State	16
60	Davis, Rob	LS	6-3	285	12/10/68	Shippensburg	16
62	Rivera, Marco	G	6-4	310	04/26/72	Penn State	16
65	Tauscher, Mark	T	6-4	320	06/17/77	Wisconsin	16
67	Ruegamer, Grey	C/G	6-4	310	06/11/76	Arizona State	15
68	Wahle, Mike	G	6-6	310	03/29/77	Navy	16
71	Barry, Kevin	T	6-4	325	07/20/79	Arizona	16
74	Kampman, Aaron	DE	6-4	287	11/30/79	Iowa	12
75	Jackson, Grady	DT	6-2	350	01/21/73	Knoxville	8
76	Clifton, Chad	T	6-5	327	06/26/76	Tennessee	16
78	Sands, Terdell	DT	6-7	340	10/31/79	Tennessee-Chattanooga	1
79	Spriggs, Marcus	T/G	6-3	310	05/30/74	Houston	2
80	Driver, Donald	WR	6-0	185	02/02/75	Alcorn State	15
81	Jackson, Chris	WR	6-2	204	02/26/75	Washington State	1
83	Chatman, Antonio	WR/KR	5-9	177	02/12/79	Cincinnati	16
84	Walker, Javon	WR	6-3	210	10/14/78	Florida State	16
85	Bailey, Karsten	WR	6-0	205	04/26/77	Auburn	1
85	Walls, Wesley	TE	6-5	240	03/26/66	Mississippi	14
86	Freeman, Antonio	WR	6-1	198	05/27/72	Virginia Tech	15
87	Martin, David	TE	6-4	260	03/13/79	Tennessee	16
88	Franks, Bubba	TE	6-6	260	01/06/78	Miami (FL)	16
89	Ferguson, Robert	WR	6-1	209	12/17/79	Texas A&M	15
90	Nwokorie, Chukie	DE	6-3	288	07/10/75	Purdue	16
91	Johnson, Joe	DE	6-4	275	07/11/72	Louisville	6
93	Brown, Gilbert	DT	6-2	340	02/22/71	Kansas	14
94	Gbaja-Biamila, Kabeer	DE	6-4	253	09/24/77	San Diego State	16
95	Walker, Rod	DT	6-3	320	02/04/76	Troy State	7
96	Smith, Larry	DT/DE	6-5	310	12/04/74	Florida State	10
97	Hunt, Cletidus	DE/DT	6-4	299	01/02/76	Kentucky State	16
98	Peterson, Kenny	DT	6-3	300	11/21/78	Ohio State	9
99	Reynolds, Jamal	DE	6-3	260	02/20/79	Florida State	5

DRAFT

Rnd	Name	Pos	Ht	Wt	College
1	Nick Barnett (29)	LB	6-2	235	Oregon State
2	(Packers traded 2nd-round pick (62) to Eagles for Al Harris and Eagles' 4th-round pick (127))				
3	Kenny Peterson (79)	DT	6-3	300	Ohio State
	(Choice from Bills for Packers 2nd-rd pick (94) and 4th-rd pick (127))				
3	(Choice (94) to Bills in deal mentioned above)				
4	(Choice (127) from Eagles in deal mentioned above; to Bills in deal mentioned above)				
4	(Choice (128) to Patriots for Terry Glenn)				
5a	James Lee (147)	DT	6-4	330	Oregon State
	(Choice from Seahawks for 5th-rd pick (165) and 6th-rd pick (203))				
5	(Choice (165) to Seahawks in deal mentioned above)				
5b	Hunter Hillenmeyer (166)	LB	6-4	240	Vanderbilt
	(Choice from Eagles for 6th-rd pick (185) and 7th-rd pick (244))				
6	(Choice (185) from Redskins for Matt Bowen; traded to Eagles in deal mentioned above)				
6	(Choice (203) to Seahawks in deal mentioned above)				
6	Brennan Curtin (212)	T	6-9	315	Notre Dame
	(Free agent compensatory pick)				
7	(Choice (244) to Redskins in deal mentioned above)				
7a	Chris Johnson (245)	CB	5-11	195	Louisville
	(Choice from Eagles for Packers 6th-round pick in 2004)				
7b	DeAndrew Rubin (253)	KR/WR	5-11	190	South Florida
	(Free agent compensatory pick)				
7c	Carl Ford (256)	WR	6-0	180	Toledo
	(Free agent compensatory pick)				
7d	Steve Josue (257)	LB	6-2	225	Carson Newman
	(Free agent compensatory pick)				

In one of the most emotional games in Green Bay Packer history, Favre threw four touchdown passes against the Oakland Raiders, the day after the quarterback's father died. A national TV audience watched the Packers win 41-7.

Did You Know?

● Favre's eighth Pro Bowl nomination tied him with Willie Wood for second in team history, one behind Forrest Gregg.

● Favre's two 400-yard passing games were his first since 1999.

● Eight players had at least 20 receptions for the Packers in 2003.

2004

Team	Games	Att	Cmp	Yds	Cmp%	Y/Att	TD	Int	Rate
Green Bay	16	540	346	4,088	64.1	7.57	30	17	92.4

Favre Highlights

A difficult year for the team still resulted in a division title as the Packers went into Minnesota in Game 15 and won a winner-take-all game for the division title. Threw for 360 yards and four TDs but the Packers still lost in a track meet at Indianapolis against Peyton Manning. Suffered a concussion against the Giants, but ran back in for a play (without clearance from the medical staff) and threw a TD pass to Javon Walker before being pulled back out of the game.

Also surpassed John Elway (4,123) for No. 2 on the all-time completions list, finishing the contest with a career total of 4,133. At Indy (Sept. 26), he became the third quarterback in league history with 4,000 career completions — joining Marino (4,967) and Elway. Also tied Unitas for the second-most four-touchdown games in league record books (17), behind just Marino (21). His four scoring throws in Colts contest also gave him 50 career games with three-or-more TD passes, he now has 51 and only Marino (62) has more. Stands second all-time with 364 career touchdown passes, leaving him just 56 behind the all-time leader, Marino (420). Established a number of milestones at Detroit (Oct. 17). Surpassed Bart Starr for No. 1 on the Packers' all-time games played list with 197 (now 199). Also moved ahead of Tarkenton (47,003) into fourth place in career passing yards and now has 47,653. His 45 career TD passes against the Lions became the fifth-most TD passes against one opponent in league history.

SCOTT BOEHM/GETTY IMAGES

Team Summary

Record: 10-6, Division Title

Playoffs: Minnesota exacted revenge for two regular season losses by rolling to a 31-17 win in Green Bay in the first round of the postseason.

Highlights: The Packers got back into the playoffs when Ryan Longwell kicked a last-second field goal to beat the Vikings on Christmas Eve, 34-31. Tragedy struck the team twice off the field, as former Packer great Reggie White passed away suddenly on Dec. 26, and Mark Hatley, the team's vice president of football operations, died of a heart attack on July 26.

GAME	DATE	OPPONENT	W/L	GB	Op.	LOCATION
1.	09-13-04	Carolina Panthers	Win	24	14	Away
2.	09-19-04	Chicago Bears	Loss	10	21	Home
3.	09-26-04	Indianapolis Colts	Loss	31	45	Away
4.	10-03-04	New York Giants	Loss	7	14	Home
5.	10-11-04	Tennessee Titans	Loss	27	48	Home
6.	10-17-04	Detroit Lions	Win	38	10	Away
7.	10-24-04	Dallas Cowboys	Win	41	20	Home
8.	10-31-04	Washington Redskins	Win	28	14	Away
9.	11-14-04	Minnesota Vikings	Win	34	31	Home
10.	11-21-04	Houston Texans	Win	16	13	Away
11.	11-29-04	St. Louis Rams	Win	45	17	Home
12.	12-05-04	Philadelphia Eagles	Loss	17	47	Away
13.	12-12-04	Detroit Lions	Win	16	13	Home
14.	12-19-04	Jacksonville Jaguars	Loss	25	28	Home
15.	12-24-04	Minnesota Vikings	Win	34	31	Away
16.	01-02-05	Chicago Bears	Win	31	14	Away
17.	01-09-05	Minnesota Vikings	Loss	17	31	Home

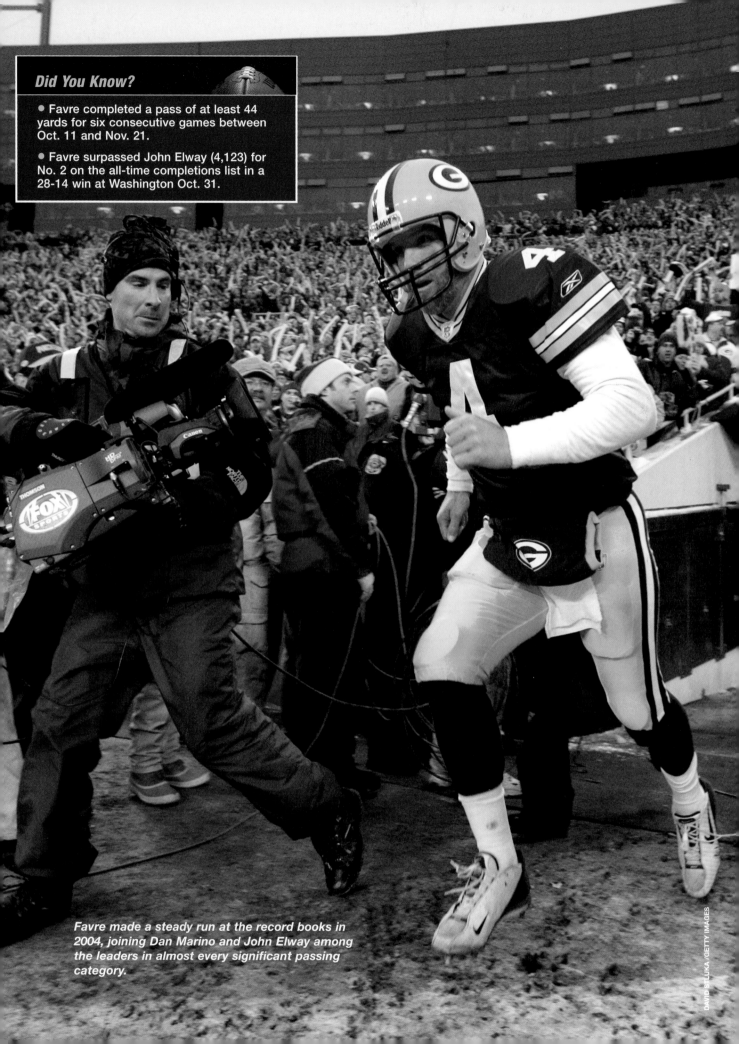

Did You Know?

- Favre completed a pass of at least 44 yards for six consecutive games between Oct. 11 and Nov. 21.

- Favre surpassed John Elway (4,123) for No. 2 on the all-time completions list in a 28-14 win at Washington Oct. 31.

Favre made a steady run at the record books in 2004, joining Dan Marino and John Elway among the leaders in almost every significant passing category.

2004

ROSTER

DAVID STLUKA/GETTY IMAGES

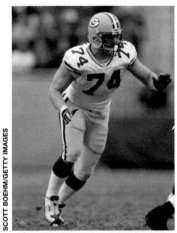

SCOTT BOEHM/GETTY IMAGES

JEFF GROSS/GETTY IMAGES

No	Name	Pos	Ht	Wt	DOB	College	G
4	Favre, Brett	QB	6-2	224	10/10/69	Southern Mississippi	16
7	O'Sullivan, J.T.	QB	6-2	220	08/25/79	UC-Davis	1
8	Longwell, Ryan	K	6-0	202	08/16/74	California	16
9	Barker, Bryan	P	6-1	205	06/28/64	Santa Clara	16
13	Kight, Kelvin	WR	6-0	209	07/02/82	Florida	1
16	Nall, Craig	QB	6-3	228	04/21/79	Northwestern (LA) State	5
18	Pederson, Doug	QB	6-3	220	01/31/68	Northeast Louisiana	4
20	Jackson, James	RB	5-10	215	08/04/76	Miami (FL)	1
21	Jue, Bhawoh	CB/S	6-0	199	05/24/79	Penn State	16
22	Luchey, Nick	FB	6-2	273	03/30/77	Miami (FL)	16
23	Roman, Mark	S	5-11	200	03/26/77	Louisiana State	16
24	Thomas, Joey	CB	6-1	195	08/29/80	Montana State	14
25	Whitley, James	DB	5-11	190	05/13/79	Michigan	6
26	Horton, Jason	CB	6-0	193	02/16/80	North Carolina A&T	14
27	Hawthorne, Michael	S/CB	6-3	204	01/26/77	Purdue	16
28	Carroll, Ahmad	CB	5-10	185	08/04/83	Arkansas	14
29	Fuller, Curtis	S	5-11	191	07/25/78	Texas Christian	1
30	Green, Ahman	RB	6-0	218	02/16/77	Nebraska	15
31	Harris, Al	CB	6-1	185	12/07/74	Texas A&M-Kingsville	16
32	Williams, Walt	RB	6-1	206	09/08/77	Grambling State	1
33	Henderson, William	FB	6-1	251	02/19/71	North Carolina	16
34	McKenzie, Mike	CB	6-0	194	04/26/76	Memphis	1
40	Fisher, Tony	RB	6-1	222	10/12/79	Notre Dame	16
42	Sharper, Darren	DB	6-2	210	11/03/75	William & Mary	15
44	Davenport, Najeh	FB	6-1	250	02/08/79	Miami (FL)	11
48	Leach, Vonta	FB	6-0	246	11/06/81	East Carolina	6
50	Navies, Hannibal	LB	6-3	249	07/19/77	Colorado	15
51	Marshall, Torrance	LB	6-2	255	06/12/77	Oklahoma	9
53	Lenon, Paris	LB	6-2	245	11/26/77	Richmond	16
54	Josue, Steve	LB	6-2	230	04/05/80	Carson-Newman	4
55	Rogers, Nick	LB	6-2	251	05/31/79	Georgia Tech	16
56	Barnett, Nick	LB	6-2	233	05/27/81	Oregon State	16
58	Flanagan, Mike	C	6-5	297	11/10/73	UCLA	3
59	Diggs, Na'il	LB	6-4	237	07/08/78	Ohio State	14
60	Davis, Rob	LS	6-3	283	12/10/68	Shippensburg	16
62	Rivera, Marco	G	6-4	307	04/26/72	Penn State	16
63	Wells, Scott	C	6-2	300	01/17/81	Tennessee	5
64	Lee, James	DT	6-5	325	03/12/80	Oregon State	9
65	Tauscher, Mark	T	6-4	320	06/17/77	Wisconsin	16
67	Ruegamer, Grey	C/G	6-4	305	06/11/76	Arizona State	15
68	Wahle, Mike	G	6-6	304	03/29/77	Navy	16
71	Barry, Kevin	T	6-4	335	07/20/79	Arizona	13
72	Bedell, Brad	T/G	6-4	306	02/12/77	Colorado	4
74	Kampman, Aaron	DE	6-4	284	11/30/79	Iowa	16
75	Jackson, Grady	DT	6-2	340	01/21/73	Knoxville	10
76	Clifton, Chad	T	6-5	330	06/26/76	Tennessee	16
77	Jenkins, Cullen	DT/DE	6-3	292	01/20/81	Central Michigan	16
80	Driver, Donald	WR	6-0	192	02/02/75	Alcorn State	16
81	Thurman, Andrae	WR	5-11	192	10/25/80	Southern Oregon	2
82	Steele, Ben	TE	6-5	250	05/27/78	Mesa State	15
83	Chatman, Antonio	WR/KR	5-9	184	02/12/79	Cincinnati	16
84	Walker, Javon	WR	6-3	215	10/14/78	Florida State	16
85	McHugh, Sean	TE	6-5	262	05/27/82	Penn State	1
87	Martin, David	TE	6-4	260	03/13/79	Tennessee	9
88	Franks, Bubba	TE	6-6	265	01/06/78	Miami (FL)	16
89	Ferguson, Robert	WR	6-1	210	12/17/79	Texas A&M	13
90	Cole, Colin	DT	6-2	320	06/24/80	Iowa	3
91	Truluck, R-Kal	DE	6-4	260	09/30/77	SUNY Cortland	14
94	Gbaja-Biamila, Kabeer	DE	6-4	252	09/24/77	San Diego State	16
96	Smith, Larry	DT	6-5	310	12/04/74	Florida State	3
97	Hunt, Cletidus	DT	6-4	310	01/02/76	Kentucky State	16
98	Peterson, Kenny	DT/DE	6-3	295	11/21/78	Ohio State	9
99	Williams, Corey	DE/DT	6-4	310	08/17/80	Arkansas State	12

DRAFT

Rnd	Name	Pos	Ht	Wt	College
1	Ahmad Carroll (25)	CB	5-10	193	Arkansas
2	Packers traded the 55th overall pick (24th pick; 2nd round) to the Jacksonville Jaguars for the 70th overall pick (7th pick; 3rd round) and the 102nd overall pick (6th pick; 4th round).				
3a	Joey Thomas (70)	CB	6-1	195	Montana State
3b	Donnell Washington (72)	DT	6-6	323	Clemson
3c	B.J. Sander (87)	P	6-3	222	Ohio State
4	Packers traded the 102nd overall pick (6th pick; 4th round) and the 153rd overall pick (21st pick; 5th round) to the Miami Dolphins for the 87th overall pick (24th pick; 3rd round).				
4	Packers traded the 118th overall pick to Jacksonville				
5	Packers traded 153rd pick to Miami (from Jacksonville)				
6	Corey Williams (179)	DT	6-3	313	Arkansas State
7	Scott Wells (251)	C	6-1	300	Tennessee

By The Numbers...

18 Favre had 18 four-TD passing games, second in league history to Dan Marino's 21.

26 Favre threw a TD pass in his 26th straight game against the Bears, the longest such streak in league history.

2005

Team	Games	Att	Cmp	Yds	Cmp%	Y/Att	TD	Int	Rate
Green Bay	16	607	372	3,881	61.3	6.39	20	29	70.9

Favre Highlights

Favre led the NFC with 3,881 passing yards and added to three of his streaks – seasons with at least 20 TD passes (12), seasons with at least 300 completions (14) and seasons with at least 3,000 yards passing (14). Favre continued to battle during the season even though injuries struck two of his top three receivers, two of his top three tight ends, all four of the Packers' running backs and his starting center. In the Cincinnati game with the Packers at the Bengals' 28 with 23 seconds left, Favre dropped back – looking to tie the game with a TD pass – when a Bengals fan who had slipped past stadium security guards ran up to Favre and took the ball out of Favre's hands. In the final game of the year, a 23-17 win vs. Seattle, Favre connected on 21 of 37 for 259 yards with one touchdown and an interception. However, the highlight of the game was the fans' repeated chant of "one more year."

TOM HAUCK/GETTY IMAGES

SCOTT BOEHM/GETTY IMAGES

Team Summary

Record: 4-12
Playoffs: Missed postseason
Highlights: Ted Thompson was named Executive Vice President, General Manager & Director of Football Operations, with full authority over football decisions. The team starts the season 0-4 and staggers to a 4-12 finish, its worst in 14 years.

GAME	DATE	OPPONENT	W/L	GB	Op.	LOCATION
1.	09-11-05	Detroit Lions	Loss	3	17	Away
2.	09-18-05	Cleveland Browns	Loss	24	26	Home
3.	09-25-05	Tampa Bay Buccaneers	Loss	16	17	Home
4.	10-03-05	Carolina Panthers	Loss	29	32	Away
5.	10-09-05	New Orleans Saints	Win	52	3	Home
6.	10-23-05	Minnesota Vikings	Loss	20	23	Away
7.	10-30-05	Cincinnati Bengals	Loss	14	21	Away
8.	11-06-05	Pittsburgh Steelers	Loss	10	20	Home
9.	11-13-05	Atlanta Falcons	Win	33	25	Away
10.	11-21-05	Minnesota Vikings	Loss	17	20	Home
11.	11-27-05	Phliadelphia Eagles	Loss	14	19	Away
12.	12-04-05	Chicago Bears	Loss	7	19	Away
13.	12-11-05	Detroit Lions	Win	16	13	Home
14.	12-19-05	Baltimore Ravens	Loss	3	48	Away
15.	12-25-05	Chicago Bears	Loss	17	24	Home
16.	01-01-06	Seattle Seahawks	Win	23	17	Home

By The Numbers...

18 — Completed passes to 18 players, two more than his previous career high (16 in 1998).

181 — With a TD pass to Tony Fisher vs. Cleveland, Favre broke Elway's single-stadium mark with his 181st at Lambeau Field.

Lance Johnstone of the Vikings introduces himself to Favre during Minnesota's 20-17 victory at Lambeau. Favre threw 29 interceptions in 2005 and the Packers slumped to 4-12.

2005

ROSTER

No	Name	Pos	Ht	Wt	DOB	College	G
4	Favre, Brett	QB	6-2	222	10/10/69	Southern Mississippi	16
6	Flinn, Ryan	P	6-5	210	02/14/80	Central Florida	2
8	Longwell, Ryan	K	6-0	200	08/16/74	California	16
10	Lucas, Chad	WR	6-1	201	11/07/81	Alabama State	1
11	Sander, B.J.	P	6-4	218	07/29/80	Ohio State	14
12	Rodgers, Aaron	QB	6-2	223	12/02/83	California	3
19	Jones, Jamal	WR	6-0	214	04/24/81	North Carolina A&T	2
21	Little, Earl	S	6-1	205	03/10/73	Miami (FL)	4
23	Herron, Noah	RB	5-11	224	04/03/82	Northwestern	5
23	Roman, Mark	S	5-11	201	03/26/77	Louisiana State	16
24	Thomas, Joey	CB	6-1	195	08/29/80	Montana State	6
25	Underwood, Marviel	S	5-10	197	02/17/82	San Diego State	16
26	Horton, Jason	CB	6-0	190	02/16/80	North Carolina A&T	9
28	Carroll, Ahmad	CB	5-10	190	08/04/83	Arkansas	16
30	Green, Ahman	RB	6-0	218	02/16/77	Nebraska	5
31	Harris, Al	CB	6-1	185	12/07/74	Texas A&M-Kingsville	16
32	Lee, ReShard	RB	5-10	220	10/12/80	Middle Tennessee State	7
32	Williams, Walt	RB	6-1	206	09/08/77	Grambling State	2
33	Henderson, William	FB	6-1	252	02/19/71	North Carolina	16
34	Dendy, Patrick	CB	6-0	190	03/10/82	Rice	4
35	Gado, Samkon	RB	5-10	226	11/13/82	Liberty University	8
36	Collins, Nick	S	5-11	200	08/16/83	Bethune-Cookman	16
37	Hawkins, Mike	CB	6-1	180	07/15/83	Oklahoma	11
38	Thornburg, Jeremy	S	6-0	196	05/07/82	Northern Arizona	4
39	Fontenot, Therrian	CB	5-11	187	06/20/82	Fresno State	1
40	Fisher, Tony	RB	6-1	222	10/12/79	Notre Dame	14
41	Wishom, Jerron	CB	6-0	197	03/01/82	Louisiana Tech	5
43	Franz, Todd	S	6-0	205	04/12/76	Tulsa	5
44	Davenport, Najeh	FB	6-1	247	02/08/79	Miami (FL)	5
47	Bigby, Atari	S	5-11	211	09/19/81	Central Florida	1
48	Leach, Vonta	FB	6-0	250	11/06/81	East Carolina	16
49	Humphrey, Tory	TE	6-2	257	01/20/83	Central Michigan	1
51	Poppinga, Brady	LB	6-3	245	09/21/79	Brigham Young	12
53	Lenon, Paris	LB	6-2	240	11/26/77	Richmond	16
54	Manning, Roy	LB	6-2	245	12/04/81	Michigan	15
55	Thomas, Robert	LB	6-0	233	07/17/80	UCLA	10
56	Barnett, Nick	LB	6-2	232	05/27/81	Oregon State	16
57	Leake, John	LB	6-0	230	08/28/81	Clemson	3
58	Flanagan, Mike	C	6-5	301	11/10/73	UCLA	14
59	Diggs, Na'il	LB	6-4	240	07/08/78	Ohio State	9
60	Davis, Rob	LS	6-3	284	12/10/68	Shippensburg	16
62	Coston, Junius	G/T	6-3	317	11/05/83	North Carolina A&T	2
63	Wells, Scott	C	6-2	304	01/17/81	Tennessee	16
65	Tauscher, Mark	T	6-4	315	06/17/77	Wisconsin	16
67	Ruegamer, Grey	C/G	6-4	305	06/11/76	Arizona State	13
68	White, Chris	C	6-2	285	02/28/83	Southern Mississippi	1
70	Klemm, Adrian	G	6-4	318	05/21/77	Hawaii	16
71	Barry, Kevin	T	6-4	332	07/20/79	Arizona	16
74	Kampman, Aaron	DE	6-4	278	11/30/79	Iowa	16
75	Jackson, Grady	DT	6-2	345	01/21/73	Knoxville	16
76	Clifton, Chad	T	6-5	330	06/26/76	Tennessee	16
77	Jenkins, Cullen	DT/DE	6-3	290	01/20/81	Central Michigan	16
79	Whitticker, William	G	6-5	338	08/02/82	Michigan State	15
80	Driver, Donald	WR	6-0	190	02/02/75	Alcorn State	16
81	Thurman, Andrae	WR	5-11	192	10/25/80	Southern Oregon	10
82	Gardner, Rod	WR	6-2	215	10/26/77	Clemson	2
82	Steele, Ben	TE	6-5	250	05/27/78	Mesa State	2
82	Wallace, Taco	WR	6-1	190	04/14/81	Kansas State	1
83	Chatman, Antonio	WR/KR	5-9	183	02/12/79	Cincinnati	16
84	Walker, Javon	WR	6-3	215	10/14/78	Florida State	1
85	Murphy, Terrence	WR	6-1	196	12/15/82	Texas A&M	3
86	Lee, Donald	TE	6-4	248	08/31/80	Mississippi State	15
87	Martin, David	TE	6-4	265	03/13/79	Tennessee	12
88	Franks, Bubba	TE	6-6	265	01/06/78	Miami (FL)	10
89	Ferguson, Robert	WR	6-1	210	12/17/79	Texas A&M	11
90	Cole, Colin	DT	6-2	325	06/24/80	Iowa	16
94	Gbaja-Biamila, Kabeer	DE	6-4	250	09/24/77	San Diego State	16
96	Montgomery, Michael	DE	6-5	275	08/18/83	Texas A&M	16
98	Peterson, Kenny	DT/DE	6-3	285	11/21/78	Ohio State	16
99	Williams, Corey	DT	6-4	313	08/17/80	Arkansas State	12

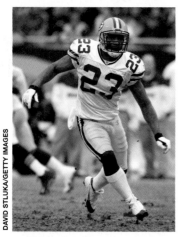

DAVID STLUKA/GETTY IMAGES

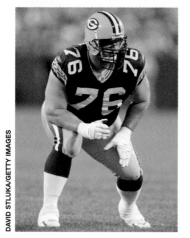

DAVID STLUKA/GETTY IMAGES

DRAFT

Rnd	Name	Pos	Ht	Wt	College
1	Aaron Rodgers (24)	QB	6-2	223	California
2a	Nick Collins (51)	FS	5-11	206	Beth-Cookman
2b	Terrence Murphy (58)	WR	6-1	202	Texas A&M
3	Packers traded the 89th overall pick to Carolina for the 115th and 126th overall picks.				
4 a	Marviel Underwood (115)	DB	5-10	205	San Diego State
4 b	Brady Poppinga (125)	LB	6-3	247	Brigham Young
4	Packers traded the 126th pick, obtained in a Day 1 trade with Carolina, to Philadelphia for 3 selections: 167th, 175th and 245th picks.				
5a	Junius Coston (143)	C	6-3	303	N. Carolina A&T

Rnd	Name	Pos	Ht	Wt	College
5	Packers trade 162nd overall pick to Kansas City for DE R. Truluck				
5b	Mike Hawkins (167)	DB	6-1	179	Oklahoma
6	Packers traded the 175th pick, obtained in a draft day trade with Philadelphia, to New England for the 195th and 246th picks.				
6a	Mike Montgomery (180)	DT	6-5	273	Texas A&M
6b	Craig Bragg (195)	WR	6-1	194	UCLA
6	Packers traded 199th overall pick to Kansas City for DE R. Truluck				
7a	Kurt Campbell (245)	CB	6-1	230	Albany State (NY)
7b	Will Whitticker (246)	G	6-5	338	Michigan State
7	Packers traders 258th pick to Kansas City for CB D. Combs (2003)				

The 2005 season wasn't a total loss: Favre led the NFC with 3,881 passing yards despite injuries to two of his top three receivers and all four of his running backs.

2006

Team	Games	Att	Cmp	Yds	Cmp%	Y/Att	TD	Int	Rate
Green Bay	16	613	343	3,885	56.0	6.3	18	18	72.7

Favre Highlights

With his performance in 2006, Favre became the NFL's all-time completions leader, surpassing former leader Dan Marino. In the fourth quarter of the Arizona game at Lambeau, Favre became only the second player in NFL history to throw for 25,000 yards in a single stadium. At San Francisco, Favre reached 200 TD passes thrown in road games, which extended his NFL record. Counting all recorded consecutive-starts streaks in NFL history, Favre is No. 3 with 236, surpassing Bruce Matthews (229, 1987-2001) at Minnesota (Nov. 12); only six active veterans across the league have played more games than Favre (240), Morten Andersen (367), Jeff Feagles (303), John Carney (260), Matt Stover (254), Chris Gardocki (243) and Junior Seau (241). The TD pass at Detroit to Greg Jennings gave Favre 10 career passes of at least 75 yards, tying an NFL record shared by George Blanda, Ed Brown, Len Dawson, Sonny Jurgensen and Norm Snead.

JONATHAN DANIEL/GETTY IMAGES

JOE ROBBINS/GETTY IMAGES

Team Summary

Record: 8-8
Playoffs: Missed Playoffs
Highlights: Aaron Kampman set a team record for most tackles by a defensive lineman with 113. The Packers finished strongly in the final month, winning four straight to end the season, including an impressive 26-7 pounding of the Super Bowl-bound Bears. Defense allowed just 23 total points in the final three games.

GAME	DATE	OPPONENT	W/L	GB	Op.	LOCATION
1.	09-10-06	Chicago Bears	Loss	0	26	Home
2.	09-17-06	New Orleans Saints	Loss	27	34	Home
3.	09-24-06	Detroit Lions	Win	31	24	Away
4.	10-02-06	Philadelphia Eagles	Loss	9	31	Away
5.	10-08-06	St. Louis Rams	Loss	20	23	Home
6.	10-22-06	Miami Dolphins	Win	34	24	Away
7.	10-29-06	Arizona Cardinals	Win	31	14	Home
8.	11-05-06	Buffalo Bills	Loss	10	24	Away
9.	11-12-06	Minnesota Vikings	Win	23	17	Away
10.	11-19-06	New England Patriots	Loss	0	35	Home
11.	11-27-06	Seattle Seahawks	Loss	24	34	Away
12.	12-03-06	New York Jets	Loss	10	38	Home
13.	12-10-06	San Francisco 49ers	Win	30	19	Away
14.	12-17-06	Detroit Lions	Win	17	9	Home
15.	12-21-06	Minnesota Vikings	Win	9	7	Home
16.	12-31-06	Chicago Bears	Win	26	7	Away

Wide receiver Donald Driver hoists Favre on his shoulders near the end of the Packers 26-7 season-ending win over the Chicago Bears at Soldier Field.

Did You Know?

● Until the Packers were blanked 26-0 by Chicago in the opener, Favre had made 222 starts without a shutout, the most in NFL history.

ROSTER

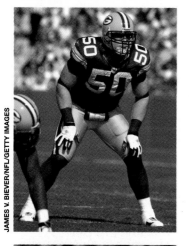

No	Name	Pos	Ht	Wt	DOB	College	G
4	Favre, Brett	QB	6-2	222	10/10/69	Southern Mississippi	16
7	Martin, Ingle	QB	6-2	220	08/15/82	Furman	1
9	Ryan, Jon	P	6-0	202	11/26/81	Regina (Canada)	16
12	Rodgers, Aaron	QB	6-2	223	12/02/83	California	2
16	Rayner, Dave	K	6-2	210	10/26/82	Michigan State	16
18	Holiday, Carlyle	WR	6-2	217	10/04/81	Notre Dame	4
19	Bodiford, Shaun	WR	5-11	186	05/04/82	Portland State	3
20	Bigby, Atari	S	5-11	211	09/19/81	Central Florida	5
21	Woodson, Charles	CB	6-1	208	10/07/76	Michigan	16
22	Manuel, Marquand	S	6-0	209	07/11/79	Florida	16
23	Herron, Noah	RB	5-11	224	04/03/82	Northwestern	16
24	Bush, Jarrett	CB	6-0	194	05/21/84	Utah State	16
26	Peprah, Charlie	S	5-11	202	02/24/83	Alabama	8
27	Blackmon, Will	CB	6-0	198	10/27/84	Boston College	4
28	Carroll, Ahmad	CB	5-10	190	08/04/83	Arkansas	4
28	Pope, P.J.	RB	5-9	218	02/26/84	Bowling Green	1
29	Culver, Tyrone	S	6-1	200	07/06/83	Fresno State	14
30	Green, Ahman	RB	6-0	218	02/16/77	Nebraska	14
31	Harris, Al	CB	6-1	185	12/07/74	Texas A&M-Kingsville	16
33	Henderson, William	FB	6-1	252	02/19/71	North Carolina	14
34	Morency, Vernand	RB	5-10	212	02/04/80	Oklahoma State	13
35	Gado, Samkon	RB	5-10	226	11/13/82	Liberty University	1
36	Collins, Nick	S	5-11	200	08/16/83	Bethune-Cookman	16
40	Miree, Brandon	FB	6-0	236	04/14/81	Pittsburgh	10
43	Dendy, Patrick	CB	6-0	190	03/10/82	Rice	12
48	Leach, Vonta	FB	6-0	250	11/06/81	East Carolina	1
49	Alcorn, Zac	TE	6-4	260	08/24/80	Black Hills State	6
50	Hawk, A.J.	LB	6-1	246	01/06/84	Ohio State	16
51	Poppinga, Brady	LB	6-3	245	09/21/79	Brigham Young	16
55	Hodge, Abdul	LB	6-0	236	09/09/82	Iowa	8
56	Barnett, Nick	LB	6-2	232	05/27/81	Oregon State	15
57	Hunter, Jason	LB/DE	6-4	255	08/28/83	Appalachian State	14
58	Taylor, Ben	LB	6-2	238	08/31/78	Virginia Tech	10
59	White, Tracy	LB	6-0	236	04/14/81	Howard	14
60	Davis, Rob	LS	6-3	284	12/10/68	Shippensburg	16
62	Coston, Junius	G/T	6-3	317	11/05/83	North Carolina A&T	1
63	Wells, Scott	C	6-2	304	01/17/81	Tennessee	16
64	Palmer, Tony	G	6-2	326	02/23/83	Missouri	6
65	Tauscher, Mark	T	6-4	315	06/17/77	Wisconsin	11
70	Walter, Tyson	T/G	6-4	300	03/17/78	Ohio State	5
72	Spitz, Jason	G/C	6-4	313	12/19/82	Louisville	14
73	Colledge, Daryn	G/T	6-4	299	02/11/82	Boise State	16
74	Kampman, Aaron	DE	6-4	278	11/30/79	Iowa	16
75	Moll, Tony	T/G	6-5	308	08/23/83	Nevada	16
76	Clifton, Chad	T	6-5	330	06/26/76	Tennessee	15
77	Jenkins, Cullen	DT/DE	6-3	290	01/20/81	Central Michigan	14
79	Pickett, Ryan	DT	6-2	322	10/08/79	Ohio State	16
80	Driver, Donald	WR	6-0	190	02/02/75	Alcorn State	16
81	Robinson, Koren	WR	6-1	205	03/19/80	North Carolina State	4
82	Martin, Ruvell	WR	6-4	217	08/10/82	Saginaw Valley State	13
83	Francies, Chris	WR	6-1	193	07/26/82	Texas-El Paso	7
84	Humphrey, Tory	TE	6-2	257	01/20/83	Central Michigan	7
85	Jennings, Greg	WR	5-11	197	09/21/83	Western Michigan	14
86	Lee, Donald	TE	6-4	248	08/31/80	Mississippi State	15
87	Martin, David	TE	6-4	265	03/13/79	Tennessee	11
88	Franks, Bubba	TE	6-6	265	01/06/78	Miami (FL)	16
89	Ferguson, Robert	WR	6-1	210	12/17/79	Texas A&M	4
90	Cole, Colin	DT	6-2	325	06/24/80	Iowa	15
93	Jolly, Johnny	DT	6-3	317	02/21/83	Texas A&M	6
94	Gbaja-Biamila, Kabeer	DE	6-4	250	09/24/77	San Diego State	16
96	Montgomery, Michael	DE	6-5	275	08/18/83	Texas A&M	11
97	Allen, Kenderick	DT	6-5	328	09/14/78	Louisiana State	2
99	Williams, Corey	DT	6-4	313	08/17/80	Arkansas State	16

DRAFT

Rnd	Name	Pos	Ht	Wt	College
1	A.J. Hawk (5)	OLB	6-1	243	Ohio State
2	Packers traded 36th overall pick to New England for 52nd and 75th				
2	Packers traded 37th overall pick received from Denver for WR Javon Walker, as well as the 139th pick, to Atlanta for the 47th, 93rd and 148th overall picks.				
2a	Daryn Colledge (47)	G	6-4	299	Boise State
2b	Greg Jennings (52)	WR	5-11	197	W. Michigan
3	Abdul Hodge (67)	LB	6-0	236	Iowa
3	Jason Spitz (75)	G	6-4	313	Louisville

Rnd	Name	Pos	Ht	Wt	College
3	Packers traded 93rd pick to St. Louis for the 109th and 183rd overall				
4a	Cory Rodgers (104)	WR	6-0	186	Texas Christian
4	Packers traded 109th pick to Philadelphia for the 115th and 185th picks.				
4b	Will Blackmon (115)	CB	6-0	198	Boston College
5a	Ingle Martin (148)	QB	6-2	220	Furman
5b	Tony Moll (165)	G	6-5	308	Nevada-Reno
6a	Johnny Jolly (183)	DT	6-3	317	Texas A&M
6b	Tyrone Culver (185)	DB	6-1	200	Fresno State
7	Dave Tollefson (253)	DE	6-4	255	NW Missouri St.

Four straight wins to end the season gave the Packers and Favre something to look forward to in 2007 – a return to glory.

By The Numbers...

6 When Brett Favre left vs. New England, it was only the sixth time in his career that he did not complete a start due to injury.

51 Including playoffs, Favre has passed for more than 300 yards in 51 games during his career.

13 Favre has 13 career rushing TDs. His TD run vs. the Cardinals was his first since 2001.

2007

Team	Games	Att	Cmp	Yds	Cmp%	Y/Att	TD	Int	Rate
Green Bay	16	535	356	4,155	66.5	7.76	28	15	95.7

Favre Highlights

Extended his consecutive games played streak in the regular season to 255 while erasing the last of Dan Marino's significant passing marks from the NFL record book. Became the league's all-time leader in passing yards (61,655) and touchdown passes on his way to a ninth Pro Bowl selection. Had one of his best seasons, completing 356 of 535 passes for 4,155 yards and 28 touchdowns with 15 interceptions. Only Warren Moon has had a comparable season at age 38, when he threw 33 TD passes in 1995. Was named *Sports Illustrated's* Sportsman of the Year after leading the Packers to the playoffs for the first time in three seasons.

JONATHAN DANIEL/GETTY IMAGES

JONATHAN DANIEL/GETTY IMAGES

GREGORY SHAMUS/GETTY IMAGES

Did You Know?

● Favre is actually on his own "receiving" list. Favre had the first pass he threw as a Packer tipped by Tampa Bay's Ray Seals. Favre caught the deflection and took a 7-yard loss.

Team Summary

Record: 13-3, Division Title

Playoffs: Hammered the Seahawks 42-20 after an opening-round bye. The Jan. 12 victory came two years to the day after the hiring of head coach Mike McCarthy. Lost 23-20 in overtime to the eventual Super Bowl Champion Giants the following week in an overtime heartbreaker in Lambeau.

The Packers reclaimed the NFC North title and finished tied for the best record in the NFC with Dallas and second-best record in the NFL behind New England. The 13-3 mark was tied for the best in team history and gave McCarthy a 21-11 mark in his first two seasons since taking over a club that went 4-12.

GAME	DATE	OPPONENT	W/L	GB	Op.	LOCATION
1.	09-09-07	Philadelphia Eagles	Win	16	13	Home
2.	09-16-07	New York Giants	Win	35	13	Away
3.	09-23-07	San Diego Chargers	Win	31	24	Home
4.	09-30-07	Minnesota Vikings	Win	23	16	Away
5.	10-07-07	Chicago Bears	Loss	20	27	Home
6.	10-14-07	Washington Redskins	Win	17	14	Home
7.	10-29-07	Denver Broncos	Win	19	13	Away
8.	11-04-07	Kansas City Chiefs	Win	33	22	Away
9.	11-11-07	Minnesota Vikings	Win	34	0	Home
10.	11-18-07	Carolina Panthers	Win	31	17	Home
11.	11-22-07	Detroit Lions	Win	37	26	Away
12.	11-29-07	Dallas Cowboys	Loss	27	37	Away
13.	12-09-07	Oakland Raiders	Win	38	7	Home
14.	12-16-07	St. Louis Rams	Win	33	14	Away
15.	12-23-07	Chicago Bears	Loss	7	35	Away
16.	12-30-07	Detroit Lions	Win	34	13	Home
17.	01-12-08	Seattle Seahawks	Win	42	20	Home
18.	01-20-08	New York Giants	Loss	20	23	Home

Two future Hall of Famers, Favre and Warren Sapp, met on the field for the last time December 9, 2007. Sapp enjoyed a good chuckle, but it was Favre who had the last laugh as the Packers bounced the Raiders 38-7 to win the NFC North Division title.

2007

ROSTER

No	Name	Pos	Ht	Wt	DOB	College	G
2	Crosby, Mason	K	6-1	212	09/03/84	Colorado	16
4	Favre, Brett	QB	6-2	222	10/10/69	Southern Mississippi	16
9	Ryan, Jon	P	6-0	202	11/26/81	Regina (Canada)	16
12	Rodgers, Aaron	QB	6-2	223	12/02/83	California	2
16	Nall, Craig	QB	6-3	230	04/21/79	Northwestern (LA) State	1
18	Holiday, Carlyle	WR	6-2	217	10/04/81	Notre Dame	1
19	Bodiford, Shaun	WR	5-11	186	05/04/82	Portland State	6
20	Bigby, Atari	S	5-11	211	09/19/81	Central Florida	16
21	Woodson, Charles	CB	6-1	200	10/07/76	Michigan	14
24	Bush, Jarrett	CB	6-0	197	05/21/84	Utah State	14
25	Grant, Ryan	RB	6-1	224	12/09/82	Notre Dame	15
26	Peprah, Charlie	S	5-11	202	02/24/83	Alabama	16
27	Blackmon, Will	CB	6-0	202	10/27/84	Boston College	9
30	Kuhn, John	FB	6-0	250	09/09/82	Shippensburg	16
31	Harris, Al	CB	6-1	188	12/07/74	Texas A&M-Kingsville	16
32	Jackson, Brandon	RB	5-10	212	10/02/85	Nebraska	11
34	Morency, Vernand	RB	5-10	212	02/04/80	Oklahoma State	13
35	Hall, Korey	FB	6-0	236	08/05/83	Boise State	14
36	Collins, Nick	S	5-11	200	08/16/83	Bethune-Cookman	13
37	Rouse, Aaron	S	6-4	223	01/08/84	Virginia Tech	11
38	Williams, Tramon	CB	5-11	182	03/16/83	Louisiana Tech	16
41	Walker, Frank	CB	5-11	196	08/06/81	Tuskegee	12
42	Wynn, DeShawn	RB	5-10	232	10/09/83	Florida	7
50	Hawk, A.J.	LB	6-1	247	01/06/84	Ohio State	16
51	Poppinga, Brady	LB	6-3	245	09/21/79	Brigham Young	16
55	Bishop, Desmond	LB	6-2	241	07/24/84	California	10
56	Barnett, Nick	LB	6-2	232	05/27/81	Oregon State	16
57	Hunter, Jason	DE	6-4	250	08/28/83	Appalachian State	16
59	White, Tracy	LB	6-0	234	04/14/81	Howard	13
60	Davis, Rob	LS	6-3	284	12/10/68	Shippensburg	16
62	Coston, Junius	G/T	6-3	313	11/05/83	North Carolina A&T	13
63	Wells, Scott	C	6-2	295	01/17/81	Tennessee	14
64	Palmer, Tony	G	6-2	311	02/23/83	Missouri	2
65	Tauscher, Mark	T	6-4	315	06/17/77	Wisconsin	16
72	Spitz, Jason	G/C	6-4	300	12/19/82	Louisville	15
73	Colledge, Daryn	G	6-4	305	02/11/82	Boise State	16
74	Kampman, Aaron	DE	6-4	270	11/30/79	Iowa	15
75	Moll, Tony	T/G	6-5	304	08/23/83	Nevada	9
76	Clifton, Chad	T	6-5	320	06/26/76	Tennessee	16
77	Jenkins, Cullen	DE	6-3	295	01/20/81	Central Michigan	16
78	Barbre, Allen	G	6-4	300	06/22/84	Missouri Southern State	7
79	Pickett, Ryan	DT	6-2	322	10/08/79	Ohio State	14
80	Driver, Donald	WR	6-0	190	02/02/75	Alcorn State	15
81	Robinson, Koren	WR	6-1	205	03/19/80	North Carolina State	9
82	Martin, Ruvell	WR	6-4	210	08/10/82	Saginaw Valley State	15
83	Francies, Chris	WR	6-1	193	07/26/82	Texas-El Paso	1
85	Jennings, Greg	WR	5-11	197	09/21/83	Western Michigan	13
86	Lee, Donald	TE	6-4	248	08/31/80	Mississippi State	15
87	Krause, Ryan	TE	6-3	244	06/16/81	Nebraska-Omaha	9
88	Franks, Bubba	TE	6-6	265	01/06/78	Miami (FL)	8
89	Jones, James	WR	6-1	207	03/31/84	San Jose State	16
90	Cole, Colin	DT	6-2	315	06/24/80	Iowa	7
91	Harrell, Justin	DT	6-4	310	02/14/84	Tennessee	7
93	Bolston, Conrad	DT	6-3	300	01/09/85	Maryland	1
94	Gbaja-Biamila, Kabeer	DE	6-4	247	09/24/77	San Diego State	15
95	Muir, Daniel	DT	6-2	298	09/12/83	Kent State	3
96	Montgomery, Michael	DE	6-5	265	08/18/83	Texas A&M	9
97	Jolly, Johnny	DT	6-3	312	02/21/83	Texas A&M	10
99	Williams, Corey	DT	6-4	313	08/17/80	Arkansas State	16

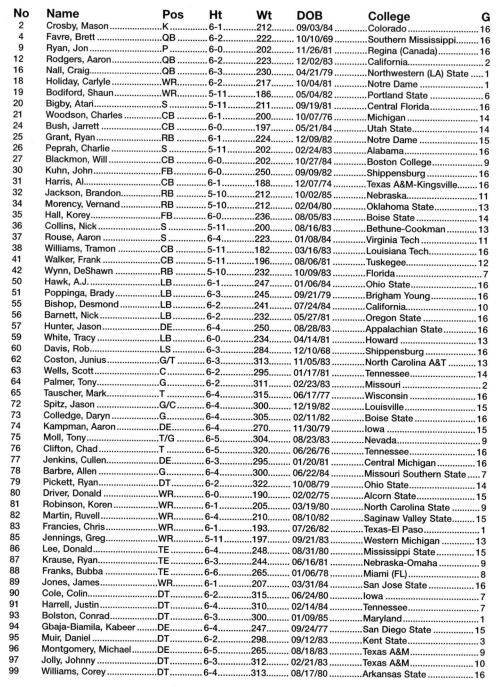

DRAFT

Rnd	Name	Pos	Ht	Wt	College
1	Justin Harrell (16)	DT	6-4	310	Tennessee
2	Packers traded 47th overall pick to NY Jets along with 235th for 63rd, 89th and 191st overall picks				
2	Brandon Jackson (63)	RB	5-10	212	Nebraska
3a	James Jones (78)	WR	6-1	207	San Jose State
3b	Aaron Rouse (89)	SAF	6-4	223	Virginia Tech
4	Packers trade 112th overall pick to Pittsburgh for 119th and 192nd overall picks				
4	Allen Barbre (119)	G	6-4	300	Missouri S. St.
5	David Clowney (157)	WR	6-0	188	Virginia Tech
6a	Korey Hall (191)	FB	6-0	236	Boise State
6b	Desmond Bishop (192)	LB	6-2	241	California
6c	Mason Crosby (193)	K	6-1	212	Colorado
7a	DeShawn Wynn (228)	RB	5-10	232	Florida
7b	Clark Harris (243)	TE	6-5	256	Rutgers

Favre was all smiles in 2007, leading the Packers to within a game of the Super Bowl while playing one of the finest seasons of his storied career.

"He's the best, bar none. Whenever God was making them, He put a little extra in him."

Cris Carter
— former NFL receiver

JONATHAN DANIEL /GETTY IMAGES

DONALD MIRALLE/GETTY IMAGES

Picture This

A Photographic Tribute to a Legendary Player

DAVID STLUKA /GETTY IMAGES

JONATHAN DANIEL /GETTY IMAGES

SCOTT BOEHM /GETTY IMAGES

"I'm thankful for all the things that this job has given me and my family. But probably the thing that I am most proud of throughout my career is that, not only myself, but my family and the people around me have just been regular people, which we are."

Brett Favre

"He was always my favorite. I've always looked up to him and admired him. He's a tough, fiery, competitor … He's a gunslinger. He may throw three picks in the first half, but he's still going to come out giving it all he's got in the next half and he may throw three touchdowns and pull the game out in the end. No matter how his body feels, he's going to come in there and compete."

Tim Couch – former NFL quarterback

"The whole season was carrying on my shoulders. Coach Mike Holmgren said 'Did you know if you didn't get in, we might not have had enough time left?' I said I never thought of that. I knew I was going to get in from the five-yard line."

–Favre, on his game-winning touchdown Dec. 18, 1994 against the Atlanta Falcons at Milwaukee

By The Numbers...

11 On Jan. 11, 1992 San Francisco offensive coordinator Mike Holmgren was named the 11th head coach in Packers history.

10 On Feb. 10, 1992 – a new hope, Brett Favre joined the Green Bay Packers and the rest is history.

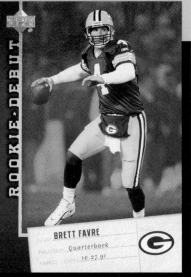

BRETT FAVRE
Quarterback
10.27.91

"Competitiveness alone won't win games, but when someone has some skill and then has competitiveness, they have a chance to be good. I knew Brett had a chance. I just did not know what he would do with it."

Irvin Favre – *Brett's father*

Vince Lombardi and Bart Star, circa the mid-1960's

"The rebirth of Favre is bad news for Bears fans. But it's great news for football, sports and, when you think about it, life."

Jay Mariotti —
Chicago Sun-Times

"I believe Brett Favre loves anybody trying to tell him he can't do something, because he'll turn around and try to do it for you. I'm watching him run that boot in for a touchdown, I'm saying, 'He can't make it, he can't make it.' And he did. He is that type of guy, and I'm fortunate to have him as my quarterback."

Mike Sherman – former Packers Head Coach

*1967 Superbowl I Packers vs Chiefs –
Bart Starr throws a pass –
Packers win 35-10*

By The Numbers...

1 It took Favre a single play to find Greg Jennings with the winning 82-yard TD heave on the first play of overtime at Denver on week 8 in 2007. The Packers won 19-13.

13 The number of victories by the Packers in the 2007 regular season – tied for best in team history.

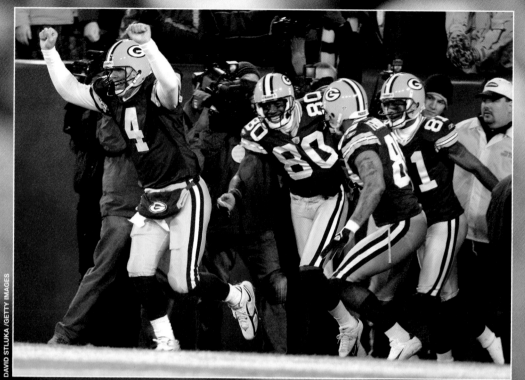

DAVID STLUKA /GETTY IMAGES

JOE ROBBINS /GETTY IMAGES

"He's one of a kind. There will never be another Brett Favre. There might be another quarterback that throws for a lot of yards and throws for a lot of touchdowns, but there will never be another Brett, given his personality and his love for the game."

Steve Mariucci
— *Former Packers quarterbacks coach*

"There was a real sense of, 'Uh oh, here he comes,' you're always worried when Brett Favre has the ball."

Jake Delhomme
— *Carolina Panthers quarterback*

Bart Starr #15 and Paul Hornung #5
circa the early-1960's

"He'll throw water on you after you've put on your coat and tie, he'll take your clothes and throw 'em in the shower or stuff 'em in an ice bag. He's big on stink bombs every once in a while, too. You would never know he is a $100 million guy. He just likes to have fun."

Mike Flanagan – former Packers teammate

"The number one sight in football thus far has been Brett Favre running down the field into the arms of his receivers. It's wonderful. America loves that. This team can play. Brett Favre is back. This guy has captured America."

Bill Plaschke
— L.A. Times

"And you know what? I don't care whether people are Packers fans or whatever, I'll reiterate what we said, rooting for Favre is like rooting for America."

Chris Berman — ESPN

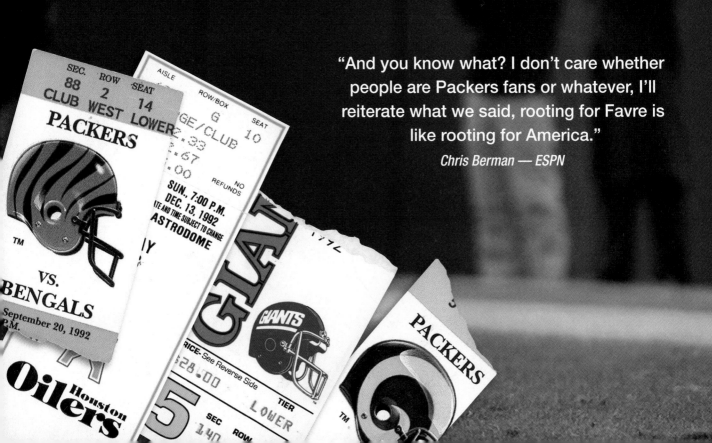

"Talented players don't always succeed. Some don't even make the team. It's more what's inside."

Brett Favre

BILL COSBY'S TRAGEDY

SMALL TOWN HEROES

How Green Bay Packers Brett Favre and Reggie White revived a team, a town and a legend

GREEN BAY
PACKERS

4

THE SPORT OF THE '60s

TWENTY-FIVE CENTS   DECEMBER 21, 1962

TIME
THE WEEKLY NEWSMAGAZINE

GREEN BAY COACH
VINCE LOMBARDI

VOL. LXXX NO. 25

TODD WARSHAW/GETTY IMAGES

MARC SEROTA/GETTY IMAGES

"And having a strong family, you know we've lost some members of our family and had some setbacks, but I think a good family and kids all those things I thought at one time... you got to be kidding me... Those things are so important they enable you to go on."
Brett Favre

"If I have to be remembered because of statistics then I did something wrong along the way. I really believe that I left a lot more than that. I can't make people like me or say good things about me but I hope that I left a pretty good impact on people."

Brett Favre

In Good Hands

Favre threw them and these guys caught them
– all 5,377 completions

Donald Driver catches a first quarter touchdown pass in front of Eric Weddle #32 of the San Diego Chargers on September 23, 2007. The Packers won 31-24.

K.C. ALFRED/UNION TRIBUNE VIA GETTY IMAGES

Player	No.	Yds.	TD	Player	No.	Yds.	TD	Player	No.	Yds.	TD
Donald Driver	496	6,774	36	Donald Lee	87	973	8	Reggie Cobb	35	299	1
Antonio Freeman	426	6,589	57	David Martin	84	743	9	Jeff Thomason	34	380	2
Ahman Green	340	2,654	14	Corey Bradford	70	1,171	7	Vince Workman	33	224	0
William Henderson	306	2,322	13	Tyrone Davis	68	757	12	Mark Clayton	32	331	3
Sterling Sharpe	300	3,696	40	Antonio Chatman	67	743	5	Darrell Thompson	30	261	1
Robert Brooks	296	4,120	32	Anthony Morgan	57	730	8	Ryan Grant	30	145	0
Dorsey Levens	269	2,073	16	Terry Glenn	55	813	2	Noah Herron	28	195	2
Bubba Franks	243	2,181	29	Ed West	55	602	2	Terry Mickens	25	233	3
Edgar Bennett	236	1,881	10	Derrick Mayes	54	730	5	Koren Robinson	24	289	1
Bill Schroeder	220	3,379	19	Keith Jackson	53	647	11	Ron Lewis	22	281	0
Mark Chmura	184	2,227	16	James Jones	47	676	2	Wesley Walls	20	222	1
Javon Walker	147	2,283	19	Harry Sydney	45	357	1	Darick Holmes	19	179	0
Tony Fisher	114	841	5	Vernand Morency	44	300	0	Najeh Davenport	17	107	0
Robert Ferguson	109	1,492	12	Don Beebe	41	727	4	Brandon Jackson	15	121	0
Jackie Harris	95	1,182	6	Mark Ingram	38	461	3	Charles Lee	13	166	1
Greg Jennings	94	1,465	15	Ruvell Martin	36	568	5	Andre Rison	13	135	1

Note: *This list includes only regular-season games.*

Sterling Sharpe

Antonio Freeman

A sure-handed Donald Driver became Favre's all-time leading receiver.

Player	No.	Yds.	TD
Sanjay Beach	13	109	0
Desmond Howard	13	95	0
De'Mond Parker	13	65	0
LeShon Johnson	12	162	0
Samkon Gado	11	82	1
Raymont Harris	10	68	0
Charles Jordan	9	171	2
Carlyle Holiday	9	126	0
Andrae Thurman	9	104	0
Brandon Miree	9	57	0
Rondell Mealey	9	76	0
Kory Hall	8	49	0
Travis Jervey	8	25	0
Reggie Johnson	7	79	0
Buford McGee	6	60	0
Basil Mitchell	6	48	0

Player	No.	Yds.	TD
Terrence Murphy	5	36	0
Jeff Wilner	5	31	0
John Stephens	5	31	0
Rod Gardner	4	67	0
Vonta Leach	4	19	0
Nick Luchey	3	32	0
Karsten Bailey	3	26	0
Ryan Wetnight	3	20	0
Ben Steele	3	15	0
Kitrick Taylor	2	63	1
Roell Preston	2	23	0
Lamont Hall	2	20	0
Marcus Wilson	2	18	0
Chris Francies	2	16	0
Michael Blair	2	13	0
Aaron Hayden	2	11	0

Player	No.	Yds.	TD
Corey Harris	2	11	0
Ryan Krause	2	9	0
Jay Graham	2	6	0
Walt Williams	1	19	0
Keith Crawford	1	14	0
Mike Wahle	1	7	0
Rashard Lee	1	5	0
Bobby Collins	1	3	0
Herbert Goodman	1	0	0
Russell Copeland	1	-1	0
Brett Favre*	1	-7	0

Ball was tipped. Favre caught it.

Note: *This list includes only regular-season games.*

Favorite Plays

Of the Thousands of Plays Brett Ran in His Career, these are the Fantastic Four

BY ROCKY LANDSVERK

Brett Favre has provided Green Bay fans with so many thrills during his years with the Packers that it's almost impossible to pick out our favorites.

So we asked him to do it for us.

There have been some simple plays made difficult, impossible plays made possible, improbable plays made easy.

Some of his more amazing moments have been little flip passes to running backs, or 1-yard scrambles. The more memorable plays feature long passes, crazy runs, rocket tosses over the middle or 80-plus-yard bombs.

"I surprise myself just about every time I do something," Favre said. "I expect to do well, but a lot of things I do, I have to look back and think, 'Wow.'"

With all that Favre has accomplished, you wouldn't think it would be possible to pick out his favorite plays. But in retrospect, you can see the rationale behind his choices. Favre's favorite plays were benchmarks for his career and the Packers' ascension. They marked milestones in the Ron Wolf/Mike Holmgren era.

Most importantly for Favre, they marked an evolution in his career as he developed from gunslinger to premier quarterback. Favre is now regarded as the probably league's finest at the audible and the league's finest at reading defenses. Now as an elder statesman, Favre is finally recognized for having a keen football mind.

He's grown a lot, in many ways, since he was that impetuous player who drove Holmgren and Packers fans crazy.

"I was 22 years old when I started," Favre said. "I get mad at people who tell me that when I was a young quarterback, I couldn't handle the blitz, or that I couldn't audible. Tell me – who is in the league right now at 22 years old who's burning the league up?

"I actually started at 21 years old and did fairly well. Tell me an-

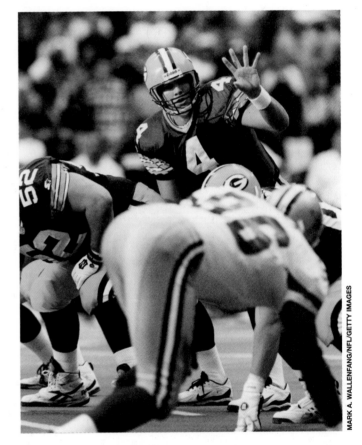

MARK A. WALLENFANG/NFL/GETTY IMAGES

other 21-year-old in the league who's doing well, who did what I did? When people second-guess me, I want them to look back and remember how young I was."

So it's not surprising that on each of the four plays he picked, Favre called an audible, made an adjustment or read the defense to perfection. He's always been able to throw a football a mile. The plays that require his film work and study are the ones that give him the most satisfaction.

"It's satisfying, but I don't think about it because it's my job," Favre said. "It's my job to put the ball in the right place at the right time."

Favre pointed out that while there are plays that he will always remember, he doesn't dream about making big plays. He thinks forward to a time when the Packers win another championship. "I don't really dream up plays," Favre said. "I don't think about particular plays. I just think about winning the Super Bowl."

KIRBY LEE/NFL/GETTY IMAGES

VERNON J. BIEVER

#4 "Freeman's Bomb"

January 31, 1997

Super Bowl XXXI was developing into one of the greatest in the game's history. The Packers jumped to a 10-0 lead, but Drew Bledsoe had led his Patriots back into the game with a pair of TD passes, and suddenly the reeling Packers trailed 14-10 at the start of the second quarter.

Green Bay needed a big play, something to turn the tide. The Packers needed their superstar player to come up with something, anything, to get the momentum back in their favor. What he came up with, on the first snap of the second quarter, was one of the biggest plays of his career.

It looked innocent enough to the untrained eye. The Packers waltzed up to the line of scrimmage with a three-receiver set. Antonio Freeman was in the slot to the right, with Don Beebe out wide. Suddenly – inexplicably in the minds of the Packers – the unprepared Pa-

triots sent strong safety Lawyer Milloy to the line of scrimmage to cover Freeman, with no safety help behind. Few fans probably noticed. Favre and Freeman saw a touchdown.

"It wasn't an audible," Favre said. "The play never changed, but the protection did, so it looked like an audible, and in many ways, it was. It was just an all-go, where you send all four guys up the field. I couldn't believe when I looked out that they had put one-on-one coverage with Antonio with a strong safety, who was bump-and-running him. Antonio will win that match-up every time."

Favre said there was eye contact and mental telepathy between himself and Freeman, who obviously saw the strong safety in front of him. The two teammates didn't make it obvious to the Patriots that they knew what was up, but they did.

"I didn't call his number out loud, but in my mind," Favre said. "I thought, 'That's where I'm going. If he doesn't win the battle, it's a dead play.' There was eye contact because we knew what was up. He won the battle. It was a mismatch from the start."

The 81-yard play became, at the time, the longest pass play in Super Bowl history. It was not only was a testament to Favre's fine throwing arm and Freeman's excellent speed, it was the culmination of years of training from Head Coach Mike Holmgren and the Packers staff. Favre and Freeman had read the coverage and made the proper adjustment. They saw the opportunity and capitalized.

It was the mark of a well-prepared team, and a Super Bowl championship-caliber quarterback.

"I was just doing my job," Favre said.

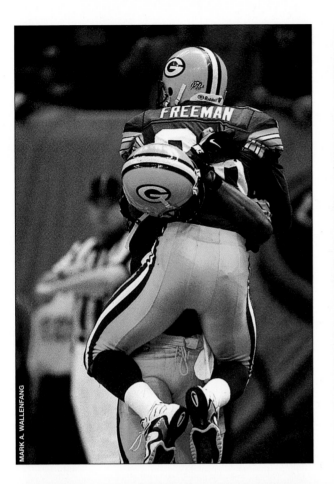

MARK A. WALLENFANG

VERNON J. BIEVER

"All Go"

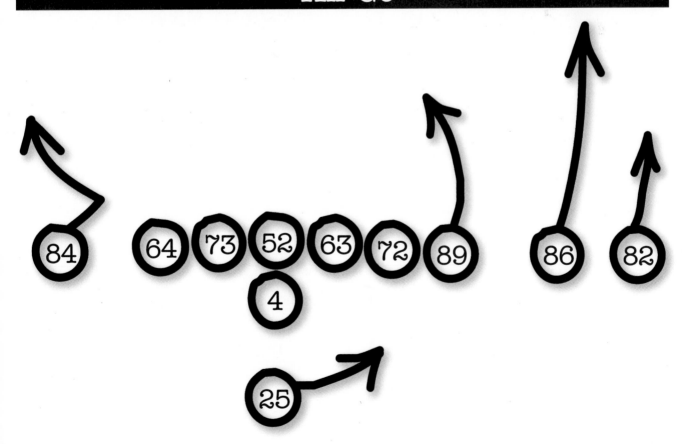

JAMES V. BIEVER

#3 "The Scramble"

December 18, 1994

It was Mike Holmgren's third season as coach, and it was beginning to appear as if the Packers were treading water. After two 9-7 campaigns and one playoff appearance, Green Bay was sitting at 7-7, needing a win against the Atlanta Falcons at Milwaukee to clinch another playoff appearance. The game had added significance for the Packers because it was their final game at County Stadium in Milwaukee, but the home team was trailing the Falcons, 17-14, and faced a third-and-two at the 9-yard line with 21 seconds left. There may not have been enough time to spike the ball if the play didn't go the sidelines or produce at touchdown — it was end zone, sideline or loss.

As Packer fans have learned to expect, Favre was about to do things his own way. With a pass rusher in his face and no receivers open, he started running, not exactly conventional fare when you're out of timeouts. But that was Brett Favre at his finest.

"That play is designed to throw to one of four guys," Favre said. "Not any one in particular – it's just a read. The right tackle had gotten beat a little bit, so his man was putting a lot of pressure on me. I stepped

> **"I realized that I had a path to run, but I had to score. It was all or nothing. There were several guys chasing me who were faster than me, but at that particular time I was running pretty fast."**

back to get outside of him, still looking downfield.

"I realized that I had a path to run, but I had to score. It was all or nothing. I was fortunate to get in because there were several guys chasing me who were faster than me, but at that particular time I was running pretty fast."

The Packers went 9-7 for the third straight season and made the playoffs for the second straight year. A loss against Atlanta could have been devastating, not only for that season, but for the development of a future Super Bowl-winning squad.

"There are a lot of things that made that play special," Favre said. "It was the final game in Milwaukee, and it clinched a playoff spot. I scored the last touchdown ever in Milwaukee, and people will remember that for a long time, including myself. I still have that game ball. It was really special."

"72 X Shallow Cross"

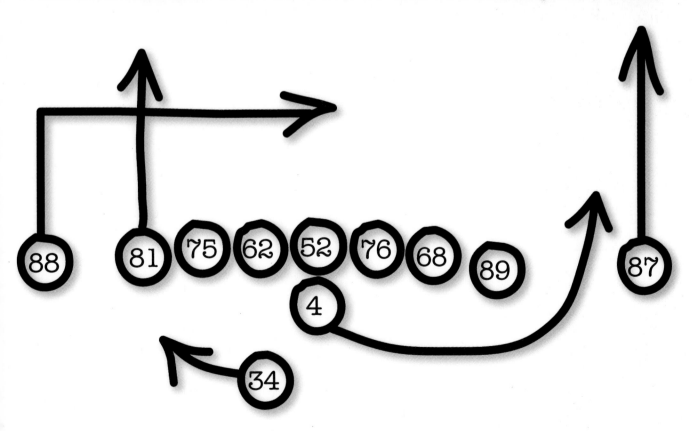

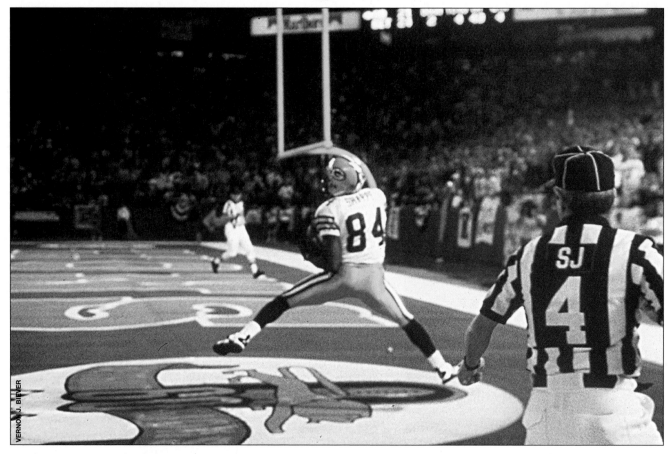

VERNON J. BIEVER

#2 "Sterling's Play"

January 8, 1994

After two decades of missing the playoffs in a regular year, and 11 years of missing the playoffs since the Packers made the second season in the 1982 strike year, The Packers went 9-7 for the second straight year in 1993 and earned a wild-card berth. Unfortunately, that meant to a trip to an unfriendly place – the Pontiac Silverdome – to play the Barry Sanders-led Lions.

Packer fans, still struggling to assess the quality and stature of the new Mike Holmgren-Ron Wolf regime, were generally skeptical about the outcome of the game. Their quarterback was only 24 years old and led the league with 24 interceptions. He was exciting but sometimes scary. He wasn't yet a full-grown NFL quarterback.

That was about to change.

Sanders was his usual self, rushing for 169 yards. Despite George Teague's 101-yard interception return, the Packers found themselves trailing 24-21 with 1:04 to play. Then Favre made a play that looked unbelievable at the time. In retrospect, it was not all the surprising.

Facing second-and-four, the Packers had their standard lineup in the game, including running backs Darrell Thompson and Edgar Bennett and tight end Ed West. The receivers were supposed to simply run square-outs, looking for the first down. But the Lions' defense spread wide to take that play away, which was just fine with Favre and his superstar receiver, Sterling Sharpe.

"That was a check at the line, but it wasn't an audible," Favre said. "The play was 25 Double Square-Out, but they played a coverage that you can't square-out on, so the receivers just fly it up the field. So both sides (Sharpe and Robert Brooks) just flew it up the field. I rolled to the left and Sterling was on the right. I don't know how I found him, but I did."

Favre maneuvered well to his left, then planted and launched a mammoth heave back to his right,. Packer fans were gasping – "What is he doing?" – until the ball landed comfortably in the arms of the wide-open Sharpe. Green Bay held on to win the game, sending it to the first of its playoff losses at Dallas.

The question football fans had for Favre was, "How did you know Sharpe was there?"

"I knew what he was supposed to do," Favre said. "Did I know he was open? No. But when I turned back to look, there was a safety to Sterling's left, but I disregarded him and just threw it up in the back of the end zone where only Sterling could catch it. He was 20 yards behind everyone else."

VERNON J. BIEVER

VERNON J. BIEVER

"25 Double Square Out"

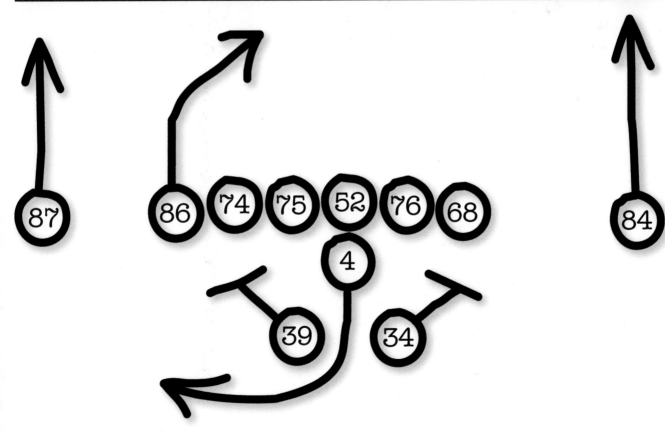

MARK A. WALLENFANG

MARK A. WALLENFANG

#1

"The Rison Play"
January 31, 1997

The Packers had waited 30 years for this moment. The Mike Holmgren-Ron Wolf era was finally coming to fruition after a few years of close calls. And suddenly the future of the National Football League exploded on one single call. An audible and a perfect strike later and the Packers led the New England Patriots 7-0 in Super Bowl XXXI.

It sent a message, not only to the Patriots but to the football world. The Green Bay Packers, with Brett Favre at the helm, were a quick-strike machine that wasn't about to take another step backward.

It was second down at Green Bay's 46 after a short run by Dorsey Levens to start the ball game on offense for Green Bay. The big play itself was simplistic in its beauty. Andre Rison, who had been acquired at midseason with this play in mind after Robert Brooks was lost for the season with a knee injury, started from the left end, put a fake on the defensive back and sprinted into the secondary, with no safeties in sight. Favre dropped a beautiful pass right on the money on his first pass of the game.

> ### "It made me look like I knew what I was doing. That was the single play that put us over the top."

Rison was gone, and so were any fears that Packer fans had that this team might have just been a dream.

"That was an audible at the line because there was no free safety. It was a blitz," Favre said. "It was an all-out blitz. That was satisfying because that's what we had studied and what I had prepared for. When I got that opportunity, there were several plays that I had the opportunity to call, but that was the one I thought would be the most appropriate, and it worked out. It made me look like I knew what I was doing."

The quick 7-0 lead on the 54-yard pass play became necessary, because New England put enough points on the board to win many games. But Favre's 246 yards passing and two touchdowns helped give the Packers their first Super Bowl win since the 1967 season, 35-21, in front of thousands of Packer fans at the New Orleans Superdome.

After the play, a jubilant Favre took off his helmet and raced jubilantly off the field, as if the Packers had already won the game. In many ways, they had.

"That was the single play that put us over the top," Favre said.

"74 Razor"

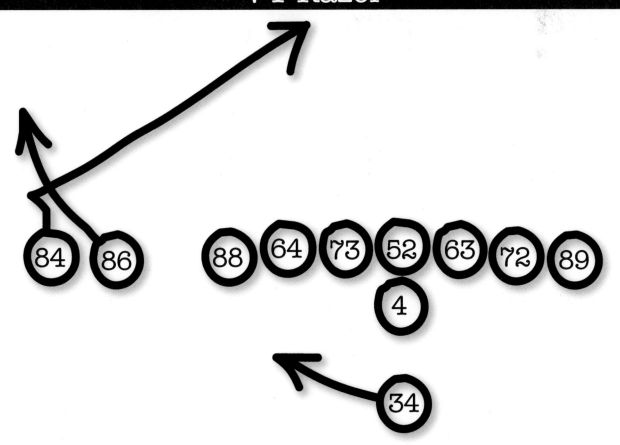

From bobbleheads to autographed footballs, Favre memorabilia is in demand

COMPILED BY TOM HULTMAN & CHRIS NERAT

SINGLE-SIGNED ITEMS

Football	$175
Authenticated football	300
Photo	50
Authenticated Photo	150
Signed mini helmet	150
Authenticated mini helmet	220
Signed full-size helmet	350
Authenticated full-size helmet	600
1996 Green Bay team-signed football	500
1996 Green Bay team-signed helmet	900
1997 Green Bay team-signed football	275
1997 Green Bay team-signed helmet	550

BOBBLEHEADS

Alexander Global green jersey, blue base	25
Alexander Global green jersey, green base	25
SAM with green jersey	125
SAM with white jersey	75
2002 Forever Collectibles	25
2002 Pacific Heads Up	50
2002 Upper Deck Playmakers	15
2003 Forever Collectibles Pro Bowl	25

2003 Forever Collectibles Bobble Mates with Ahman Green	30
2003 Forever Collectibles Bobble Mates with Bubba Franks	30
2003 Forever Collectibles Game Look (5,000 issued)	20
2003 Forever Collectibles 18-inch (100 issued)	130
2003 Forever Collectibles 36-inch (100 issued)	350
2003 Upper Deck Classic (600)	50
2004 Forever Collectibles 8-inch Ticket Base (5,000)	20
2004 Forever Collectibles Bobble Mates with Ahman Green (5,000)	35
2004 Forever Collectibles Bobble Mates with Mike Sherman (5,000)	35
2004 Forever Collectibles 18-inch Ticket Base (100)	140
2004 Forever Collectibles 36-inch (100)	350
2004 Forever Collectibles 4-inch Rocker	10
2004 Forever Collectibles 8-inch Pro Bowl (5,000), with A. Green	40
2004 Forever Collectibles 8-inch Pro Bowl (5,000)	25
2004 Forever Collectibles NCAA Standouts, S. Mississippi	25

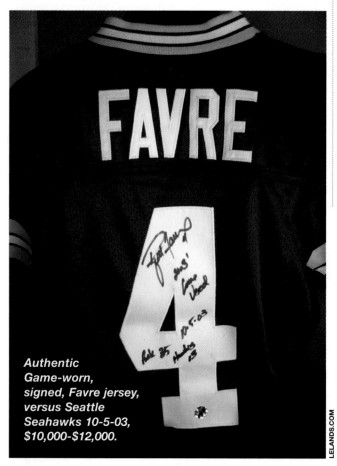

Authentic Game-worn, signed, Favre jersey, versus Seattle Seahawks 10-5-03, $10,000-$12,000.

LELANDS.COM

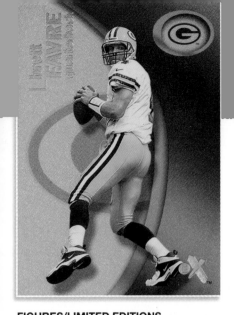
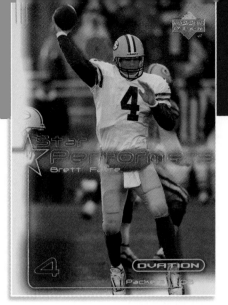
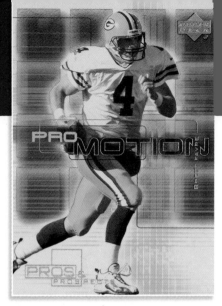

FIGURES/LIMITED EDITIONS

Art of Sport (1,500).. 220
Art of Sport autographed (500)... 470
Art of Sport Artist Proof (10)... 2,000
Bradford Exchange Plates, Leader of the Pack 30
Bradford Exchange Plates, 3 Degrees to Victory....................... 30
Bradford Exchange Plates, Titletown...................................... 30
Bradford Exchange Plates, Pack Is Back................................. 30
Bradford Exchange Plates, Touchdown.................................... 30
Bradford Exchange Plates, Collector plate............................... 30
Danbury Mint Figure.. 65
1996 Headliners figurine 12
1997 Headliners figurine 10
1997 Headliners Throwback figurine.. 35
1998 Headliners figurine 10
1998 Headliners NFL in the Trenches figurine........................... 20
1998 Headliners NFL Sideline QBs figurine.............................. 20
1999 Headliners NFL two-pack Present Super Bowl, with Elway 45
1994 Highland Mint Topps bronze card (714)........................... 115
1994 Highland Mint Topps silver card (110)............................ 325
1995 Highland Mint silver medallion (7,500)............................. 50
1995 Highland Mint Score bronze card (1,500) 105
1996 Highland Mint Score silver card (250)............................ 300
1996 Highland Mint bronze medallion (25,000) 30
1996 Highland Mint silver medallion (4,500)............................. 60
1996 Highland Mint gold signature (1,500).............................. 100
1997 Highland Mint silver MVP medallion (3,500) 40
1997 Highland Mint Magnum bronze (2,500)............................. 55
1997 Highland Mint Magnum silver (500)................................ 150
1997 Highland Mint Magnum gold (250) 250
1997 Highland Mint bronze Team Coins with Reggie White
    and Mark Chmura 45
1999 Highland Mint Photo-Mint (2,500) 80
2001 Hallmark Figure 20
2001 Highland Mint Photo-Mint autographed 200
2003 Highland Mint game-used Photo-Mint autographed 200
2003 Highland Mint game-used Photo-Mint with Bart Starr (patch) 200
2004 Highland Mint Photo-Mint (250) 80
1994 Kenner Starting Lineup 120
1995 Kenner Starting Lineup 40
1996 Kenner Starting Lineup (Shopko) 35
1997 Kenner Starting Lineup 20
1997 Kenner Starting Lineup Classic Doubles 30
1997 Kenner Starting Lineup Gridiron Greats............................. 30
1998 Kenner Starting Lineup 14
1998 Kenner Starting Lineup Cincinnati Convention 35
1998 Kenner Starting Lineup 12-inch figure 30
1999 Kenner Starting Lineup 10
1999 Kenner Starting Lineup QB Club 23
1999 Kenner Starting Lineup 12-inch figure 25
2000 Kenner Starting Lineup 12
2000 Kenner Starting Lineup Classic Doubles 20
2000 Kenner Starting Lineup Football Elite 20

First Favre win full ticket Vs. Bengals

First Favre start full ticket Vs. Steelers

Brett Favre signed and framed photo, $300.

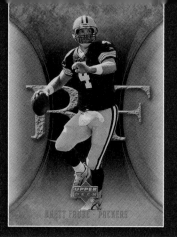

2000 Wheaties Series I figure	20
2002 McFarlane Series 4 green jersey/sleeves	18
2002 McFarlane Series 4 white jersey/white sleeves	90
2002 McFarlane Series 4 white jersey/green sleeves	40
2003 McFarlane Series 6 Falcons jersey with handwarmer	220
2003 McFarlane Series 6 Falcons jersey, no handwarmer	45
2003 McFarlane Series 7 green jersey	15
2003 McFarlane Series 7 white jersey	25
2003 McFarlane 12-inch Series 1, green jersey	35
2003 McFarlane 2-pack Favre vs. Brian Urlacher	35
2004 McFarlane 12-inch Series 2 (Series 1 packaging), white jersey, dull pants	45
2004 McFarlane 12-inch Series 2 (Series 1 packaging), white jersey, shiny pants	45
2003 Memory Co. Gridiron Greats	60
2003 Upper Deck NFL GameBreakers	25

GAME-WORN EQUIPMENT

Misc game-worn Packers jersey 7,500-10,000

PUBLICATIONS

1993 *Green Bay Packers Yearbook*	10
1996 *Green Bay Packers Yearbook*	10
1999 *Green Bay Packers Yearbook*, with Ray Rhodes, others	10
2001 *Green Bay Packers Yearbook*	10
1993 *Green Bay Packers Media Guide*	20
1998 *Green Bay Packers Media Guide*	20
2002 *Green Bay Packers Media Guide*	20
ESPN Magazine, Nov. 1, 1999	3
1993 *Street and Smith*, with Joe Montana	15
1995 *Street and Smith*, with Warren Moon	12
1996 *Street and Smith*	12
Inside Sports, February 1998, with Steve Young and John Elway	4
Sport, August 1996, with Dan Marino, Junior Seau, Emmitt Smith	6
Sport, February 1997, with John Elway	8
Sport, Aug. 1997	8
Sports Illustrated, Jan. 15, 1996	8
Sports Illustrated, Dec. 16, 1996	8
Sports Illustrated, Jan. 27, 1997, with Mike Holmgren	7
Sports Illustrated, Aug. 17, 1998	8
Sports Illustrated, Dec. 23, 2002	6
Time, Jan. 27, 1997, with Reggie White	5
TV Guide, Jan. 25-31, 1997, with Drew Bledsoe, SB XXXI issue	4
TV Guide, Jan. 25-31, 1997, Super Bowl XXXI issue	4
TV Guide, Jan. 24-30, 1998, Super Bowl XXXII issue	4
TV Guide, Sept. 5-11, 2004	cover price
Favre: For the Record book, by Brett Favre, Chris Havel (1997), Doubleday	17

MISCELLANEOUS

1994 Action Packed Badge of Honor Pin	6
1997 Wheaties Packers Super Bowl XXXI Champs, with Edgar Bennett, Reggie White, Mark Chmura and Desmond Howard	15
1998 Wheaties 3-Time MVP regional box	15
1998 Wheaties QBs, with John Elway and Steve Young	15

Source: *Standard Catalog of Sports Memorabilia,*
Third Edition by Bert Lehman

Opposite Top Left: Unsigned Sports Illustrated ***1996 NFL Preview issue, $20.***
Opposite Top Right: Brett Favre signed Sports Illustrated ***commemorative edition, Super Bowl XXI championship, framed, $150.***
Opposite Bottom: Collection of Green Bay Packers yearbooks with Favre on cover, $60-$80.

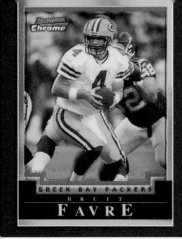

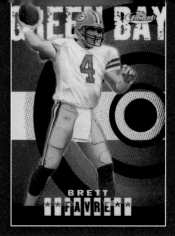

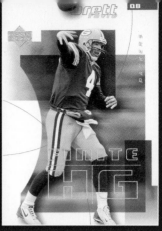

Brett Favre, Bart Starr dual-signed photo display, $700.

Above: Brett Favre signed Southern Mississippi mini helmet, $150.

Right: Regular size Brett Favre bobblehead, $20.

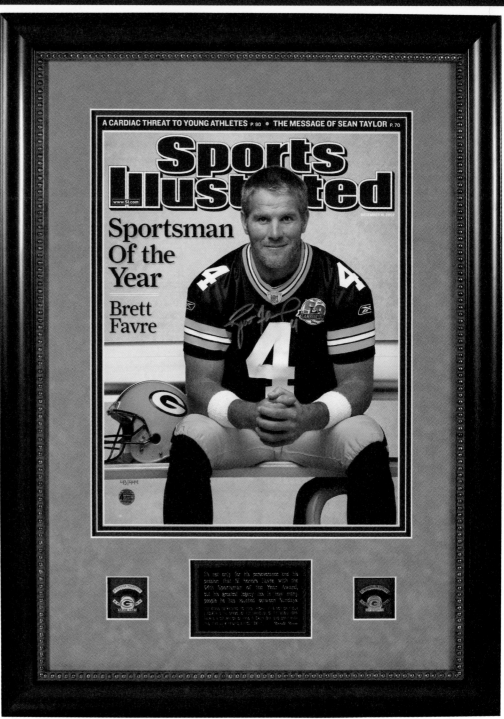

Brett Favre signed and framed, oversized Sports Illustrated "Sportsman of the Year" cover, $400.

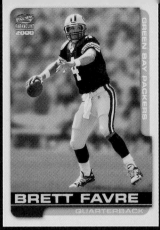

Above: Brett Favre signed authentic Green Bay Packers helmet, $600.

Right: Oversized Brett Favre bobble-head, $75.

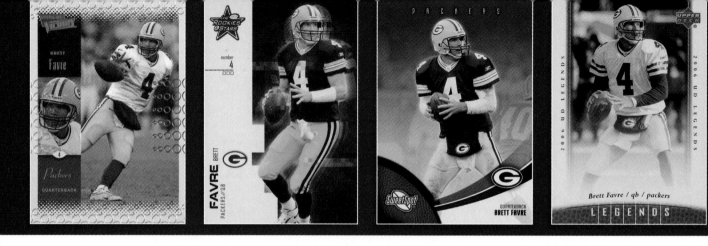

Brett Favre signed and framed "MVP Season" litho, $500.

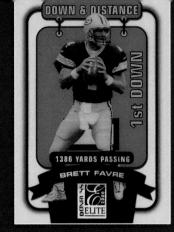

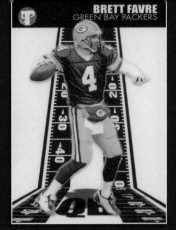

Above: Brett Favre/Bart Starr dual-signed authentic helmet, $850-$1,000.

Right: Brett Favre bobblehead, $20.

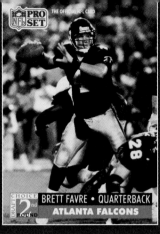

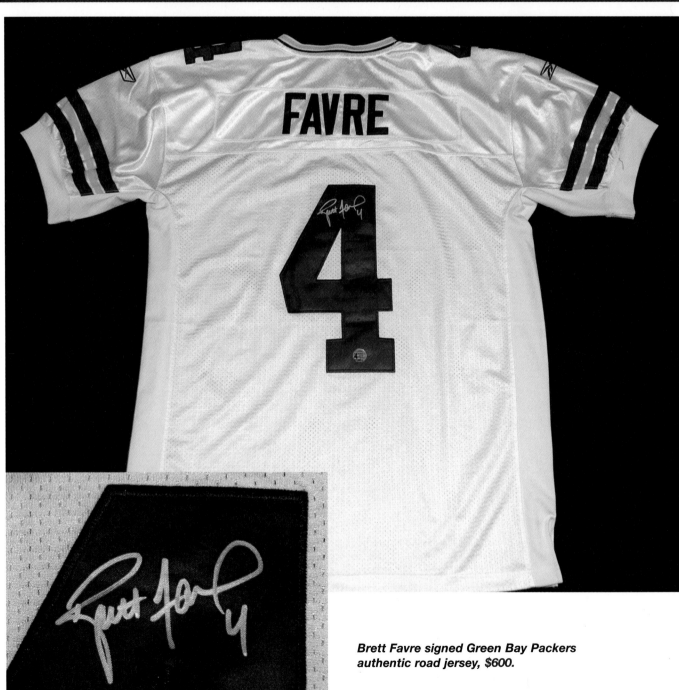

**Brett Favre signed Green Bay Packers
authentic road jersey, $600.**

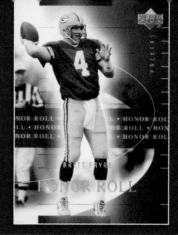

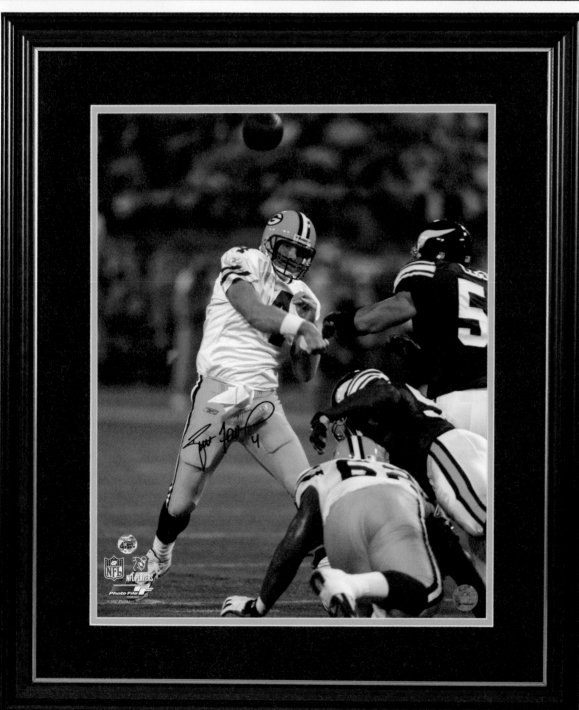

Brett Favre signed and framed photo, NFL career touchdown record pass to Gregg Jennings, individually numbered, tamper evident hologram, $300.

Brett Favre signed and framed "Game Ball" photo display, $350.

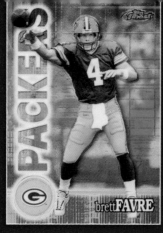

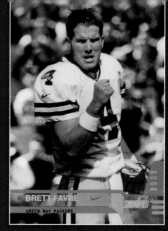

Above: Brett Favre signed Super Bowl XXXI mini helmet, $150.

Right: Brett Favre pewter bust by Brad Lorang, $125.

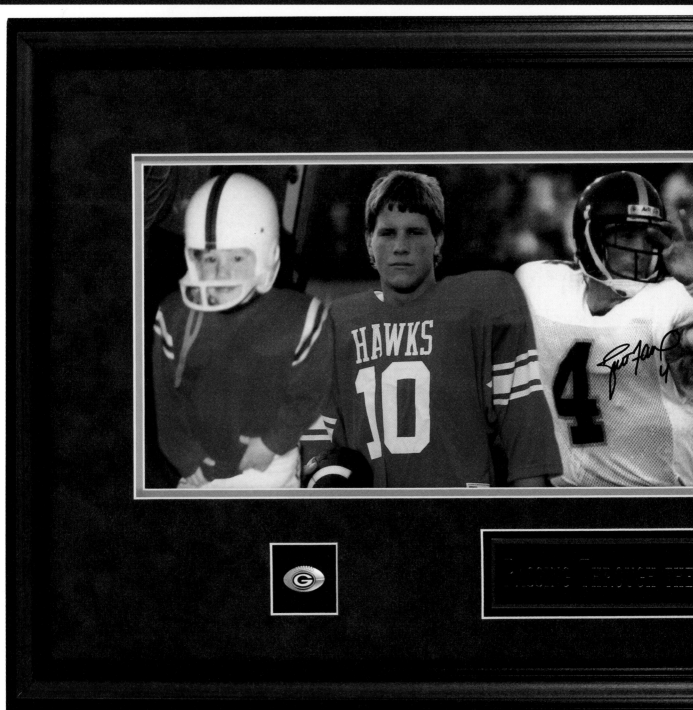

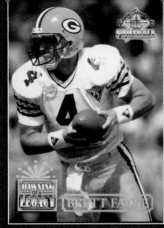

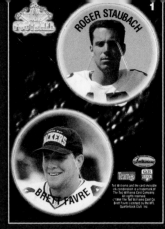

Brett Favre signed "Passing Through the Years" framed photo display, $400.

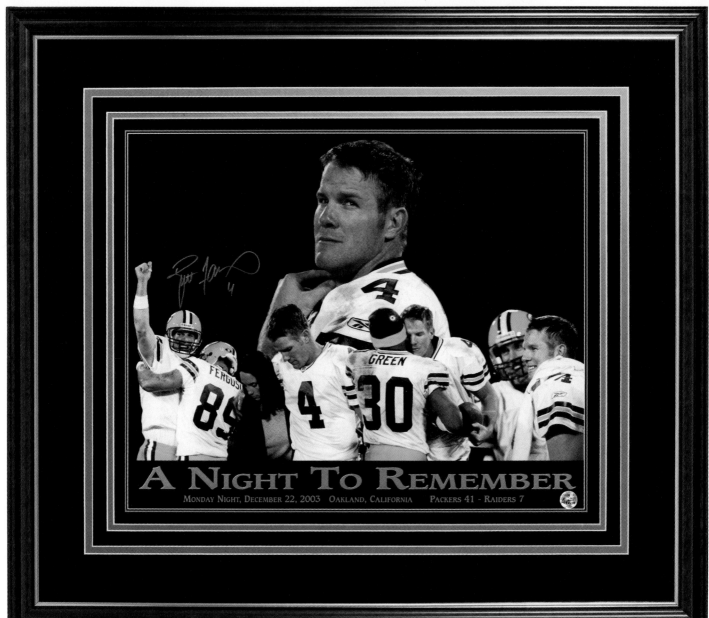

Brett Favre signed and framed, "A Night to Remember" photo display, $350.

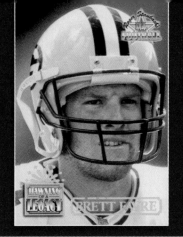

Above: Green Bay Packers Media Guide, 1998, $20.

Left and Below: Brett Favre signed first-edition autobiogrphy, Favre: For the Record, Doubleday, 1997, $150.

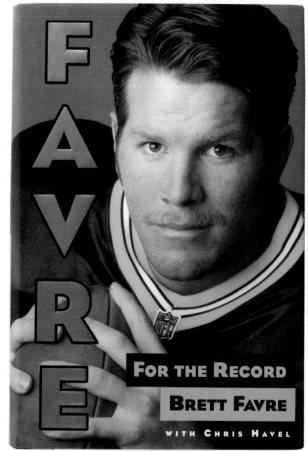

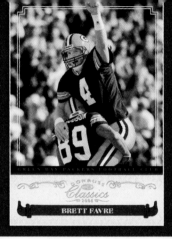
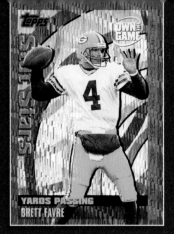

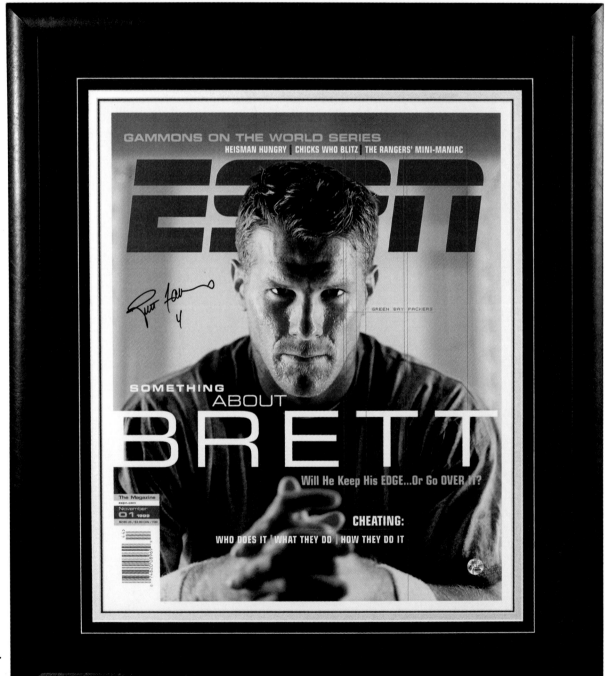

Brett Favre signed and framed, over-sized ESPN The Magazine **cover, $400.**

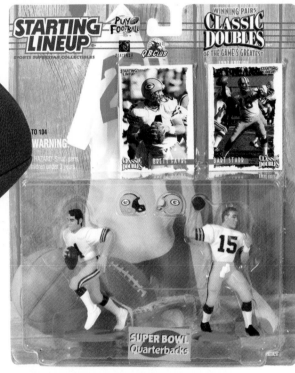

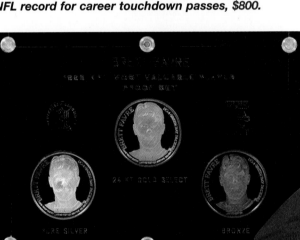

Brett Favre, Dan Marino dual-signed football commemorating NFL record for career touchdown passes, $800.

Starting Lineup, Brett Favre/Bart Starr Classic Doubles, $20.

Brett Favre 1996 NFL Most Valuable Player Proof Set, 24KT Gold Select, Pure Silver, Bronze, $80.

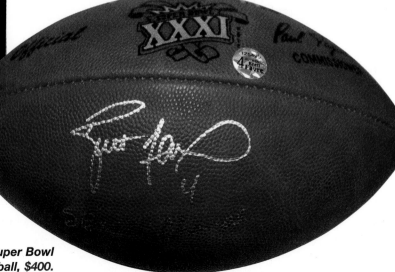

Brett Favre signed Super Bowl XXXI football, $400.

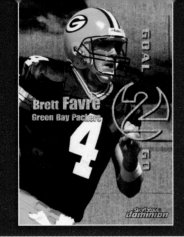

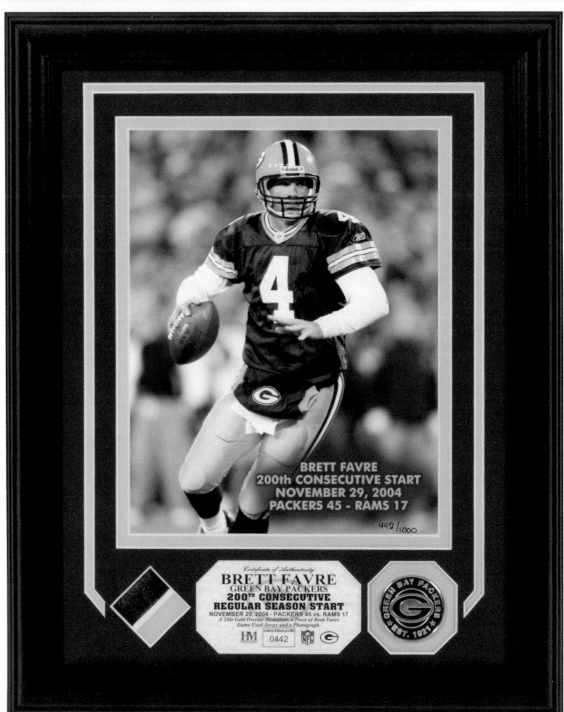

Highland Mint framed game-used jersey swatch display, $100.

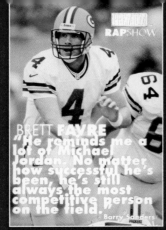
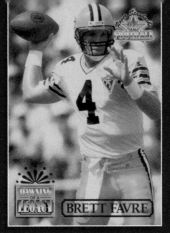

Re-Plays Series 3, Brett Favre, $15.

Above: McFarlane, Brett Favre Action Figure, Series 4, 2002, $20.

Left: McFarlane, Brett Favre Action Figure, Series 7, 2003, $20.

Re-Plays Series 3, Brett Favre, throwback jersey, $15.

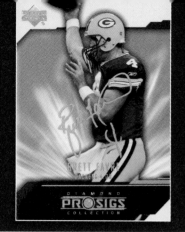

Brett Favre face mug, $10.

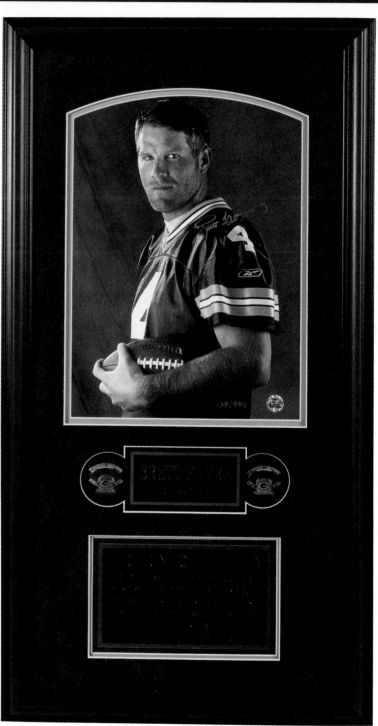

Brett Favre signed and framed photo display, $350.

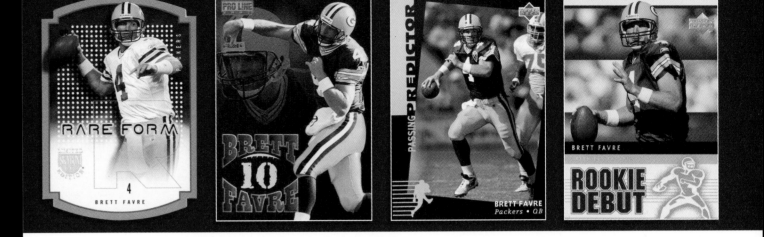

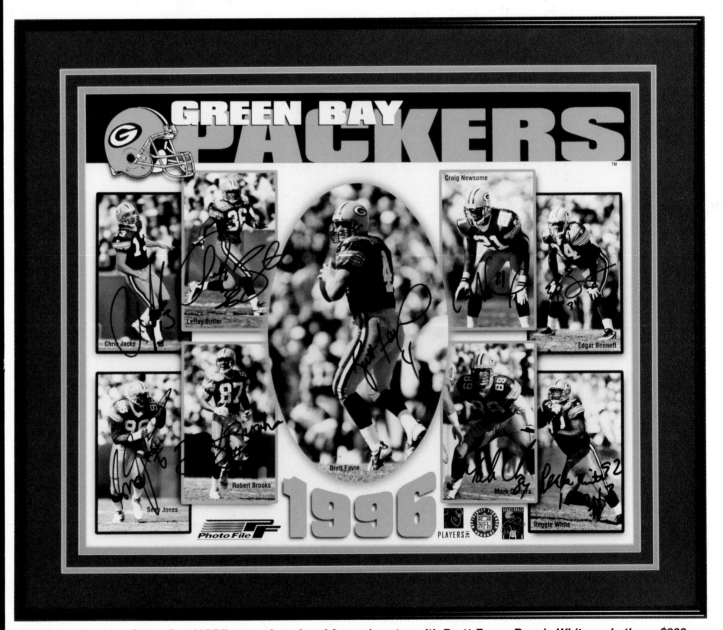

Green Bay Packers Super Bowl XXXI team signed and framed poster with Brett Favre, Reggie White and others, $800.

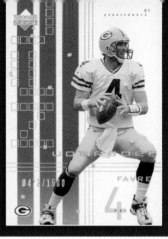

Brett Favre signed 1996 NFC Championship game program, $300.

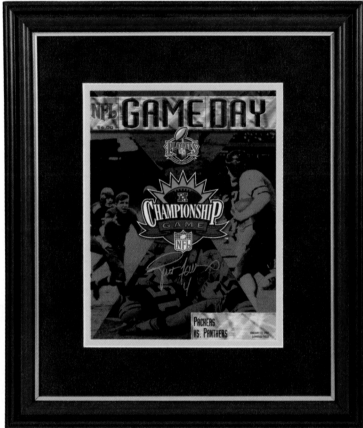

Brett Favre signed Green Bay Packers Super Bowl XXXI framed poster $200.

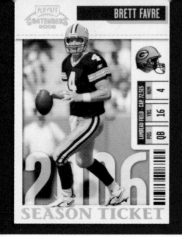

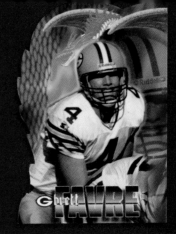

Brett Favre,
Bart Starr
dual-signed
frame display,
$700.

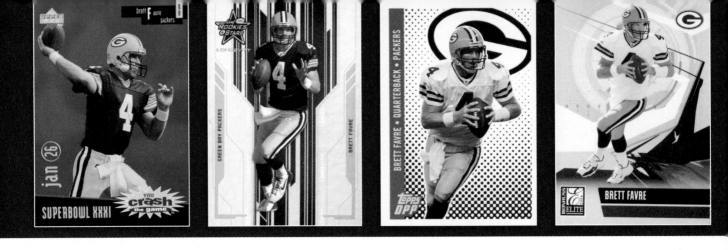

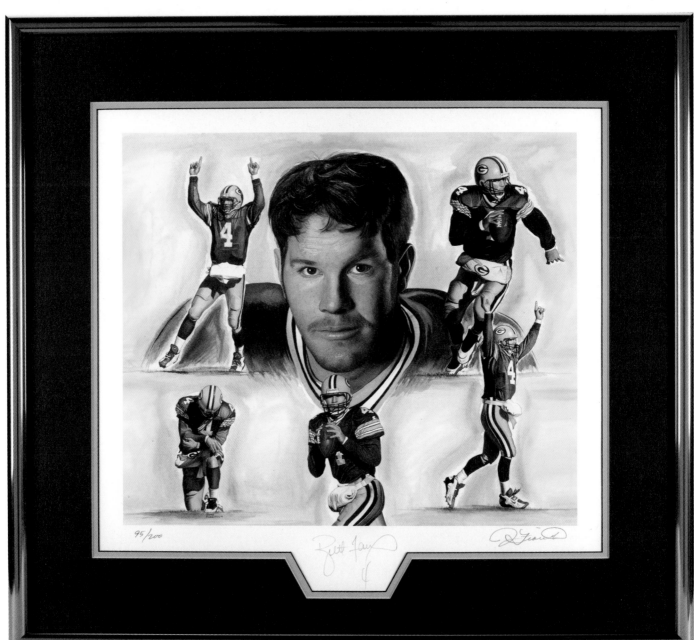

Brett Favre signed and framed litho, $500.

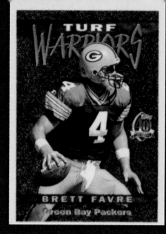

"Deal Me In" framed painting, 16x20, $150.

"Deal Me In"

The Legends of Lambeau

775/2,500

Green Bay Packers Legends posters, $25.

Special thanks to Card and Coin Corner/ Packer City Antiques, Green Bay, WI for their help.